The Art of Styling Sentences

20 Patterns for Success

Fourth Edition

by
Ann Longknife, Ph.D.
Associate Professor of English
College of San Mateo

K. D. Sullivan
Owner of Creative Solutions Editorial, Inc
Author of Go Ahead...Proof It!

Marie L. Waddell
Robert M. Esch
Roberta R. Walker

BARRON'S

All inquiries should be addressed to:

Barron's Educational Series, Inc.
250 Wireless Boulevard
Hauppauge, New York 11788
http://www.barronseduc.com

Library of Congress Catalog Card No. 2002018477

ISBN-13: 978-0-7641-2181-4
ISBN-10: 0-7641-2181-2

Library of Congress Cataloging-in-Publication Data
Longknife, Ann.
    The art of styling sentences : 20 patterns for success / Ann Longknife,
K.D. Sullivan.—4th ed.
        p.   cm.
    Rev. ed. of: The art of styling sentences / Marie L. Waddell . . . [et al.]
3rd ed. c1993.
    Includes index.
    ISBN 0-7641-2181-2
    1. English language—Sentences.   2. English language—Rhetoric.
I. Sullivan, K.D.   II. Waddell, Marie L. Art of styling sentences.   III. Title.
PE1441 .L57 2002
428.2—dc21

                                                        2002018477

PRINTED IN THE UNITED STATES OF AMERICA

19 18 17 16 15 14

Contents

Preface

The authors of the original text compiled their book to help students improve their writing style. The principles they advocated—and that have been used throughout history—of learning to write by imitating patterns, are still valid today, as shown in this revised fourth edition. They devised the idea of the book from their extensive classroom experience, and we have built on that from our own classroom and editing experience.

In her twenty-five years of teaching, Dr. Ann Longknife has taught a variety of English courses—literature, poetry, and all forms of composition courses from English as a Second Language to Critical Thinking. Ann is also a freelance editor for a number of publications, including the on-line magazine *LineZine*, and has been in love with English and its possibilities since she started reading at age four.

K.D. Sullivan, as founder and owner of Creative Solutions Editorial, Inc., a global editorial services company, has worked with, and corrected, a wide variety of writing styles in more than 100 different industries. She is the author of *Go Ahead . . . Proof It!* (Barron's, 1996), and coauthor with Michelle Goodman of the upcoming *In the Driver's Seat: A Roadmap to Freelancing*. She is also developing a book series, *Go Ahead . . . _____!*, designed to cover a wide range of specific business topics. A popular seminar leader and trainer, K.D. regularly designs and implements proofreading workshops and corporate training programs throughout the United States and Canada. She is known for producing clear, error-free written communications.

In this new edition we have expanded some of the grammar references to more nearly reflect current knowledge and usage. We have also upgraded many of the professional examples to illustrate how current writers regularly continue to use these patterns.

Although the idea of the book is to learn by imitating the patterns, that technique is only the beginning. We, as did the original authors, hope that students will find new ways of being playful or serious, dramatic or forceful as they write. Above all, we want them to take risks with patterns they've never tried before, to claim authority for their individual style, and to develop their own voice.

At Barron's, we have appreciated the gracious and professional guidance of our editor, Max Reed, in preparing this new edition. We would like to thank Diane Roth, copyeditor. Her suggestions made good sense and strengthened our presentation.

We've included a very valuable addition in this version that was absent in previous editions—an Index—to help more easily guide the student in the reference process. DQ Johnson's expertise in the indexing field is a welcome addition to any project. K.D. would also like to thank Deirdre Greene, her Creative Solutions manager, who continually keeps the business going so beautifully, allowing K.D. to concentrate on this book and the multitude of other projects she enjoys.

Ann Longknife
K.D. Sullivan

SAN FRANCISCO
JULY 2002

Introduction

Almost anyone can benefit by learning more about writing sentences. You don't have to be a student to benefit from this book; you just need the desire to write well. You must certainly want to create better sentences, or you would not be reading this page. If you already know how to write good, basic sentences but feel they still lack something, that they have no variety, no style, then this book is for you.

But how do you go about writing better sentences? The answer is simple. You learn to write better sentences as you learn almost every other skill: by imitating the examples of those who have that skill. You probably have already discovered that it is easier to master anything—jumping hurdles, doing a swan dive, or playing the guitar—if you imitate a model. Nowhere is this principle more obvious than in writing. If you are willing to improve your writing skills by copying models of clear sentences, the following five chapters will help you master the skill of writing well, with grace and style.

THE WHOLE IS THE SUM OF ITS PARTS

CHAPTER 1 briefly reviews what constitutes a sentence. If you need to review the functions of different parts of a sentence, you may need a supplementary book with a fuller discussion of sentence structure. This chapter covers the various parts of the sentence, utilizing the traditional terms you will find in the explanations of the patterns in CHAPTER 2.

SKILL COMES FROM PRACTICE

CHAPTER 2, the heart of this book, contains twenty different sentence patterns, some with variations. Study the graphic picture of each pattern (the material in the numbered boxes) and notice the precise punctuation demanded for that pattern; you will then be able to imitate these different kinds of sentences. The explanation under each boxed pattern will further clarify HOW and WHEN you should use that particular pattern; the examples will give you models to imitate; the exercises will provide practice. With these as guides, try writing and revising until you master the skill of constructing better sentences.

As you revise, take some of your original sentences and rewrite them to fit a number of these patterns. This technique may at first seem too deliberate, too contrived an attempt at an artificial style. Some of the sentences you create may not seem natural. But what may seem artificial at first will ultimately be the means to greater ease in writing with flair and style.

CLEAR WRITING COMES FROM REWRITING

Your first draft of any communication—letter, theme, report (either written or oral)—will almost always need revision. When you first try to express ideas, you are mainly interested in capturing your elusive thoughts, in making them concrete enough on a sheet of paper for you to think about them. An important step in the writing process—in fact, where writing really begins—is revision, an ongoing process. You must work deliberately to express your captured ideas in clear and graceful sentences.

COMBINATIONS LEAD TO ENDLESS VARIETY

CHAPTER 3 will give you some tips on style and show you how some of the basic twenty styling patterns in CHAPTER 2 can combine with other patterns. Study the examples given and described in CHAPTER 3; then let your imagination guide you to making effective combinations of the different patterns.

Analyze the sentences from professional writers to discover rhetorical subtleties and ways of achieving clarity, style, and variety.

IMAGINATION IS ONE CORNERSTONE OF STYLE

CHAPTER 4 will show you how to express your thoughts in imaginative, figurative language. Study the pattern for each figure of speech described there, and then insert an occasional one—simile, metaphor, analogy, allusion, personification, hyperbole—into your own writing. Or you might experiment with an ironical tone. Be original; never merely echo some well-known, ready-made cliché. Create new images from your own experiences.

UNDERSTANDING COMES FROM ANALYSIS

CHAPTER 5 contains excerpts from the works of experienced writers who have incorporated patterns like the ones described. Study the marginal notes that give the pattern numbers you have learned from studying CHAPTER 2. Then analyze something you are reading; discover for yourself how writers handle their sentences and their punctuation. Don't be afraid to imitate them when you write. You will, of course, find "patterns" (arrangements of words in sentences) that are not in CHAPTER 2 of this book. Imitate others as well as the twenty we present.

Suggestions for the Instructor

Since this method of teaching students to write by imitation may be new to some instructors, we hope this section will offer helpful and practical suggestions. For the new teacher, we want to anticipate possible questions and provide some classroom guidelines; for the experienced teacher, we hope to offer a fresh approach to an old problem: getting students to write papers that are not dull and boring for them to write or for us to read. The following pages contain some hints for ways of teaching the material in CHAPTERS 1 and 2. Additional pages addressed to students also suggest valuable ways for the teacher to present the patterns and other techniques to a class.

SENTENCE COMBINING

Concurrently with publication of the first edition of *The Art of Styling Sentences*, a number of researchers developed a teaching technique quite different from the "imitation" method described in this book—sentence combining. Introduced first by John Mellon and later developed in the work of Frank O'Hare, William Strong, Donald Daiker, and others, this technique derives from a number of sentences—usually short, simple, kernel sentences—a pattern for combining them into one or two longer sentences. Through this type of practice, the student develops syntactic maturity. The result of this method is effective skill building; students' sentences have greater variety, appear more mature and sophisticated, and illustrate how writers in the same class, working with the same kernels, are able to transform them into many different types of effective communication.

SUGGESTIONS FOR TEACHING CHAPTER 1

As we said in the introduction, CHAPTER 1, "The Sentence," does not pretend to be a complete discussion of sentence structure. The English sentence took several centuries to develop and is, as Sir Winston Churchill said, a "noble thing" indeed. There are entire books dedicated to an explanation of it; hence our coverage is minimal.

The main thing to do with CHAPTER 1 is to review with your class the important "slots" in the standard sentence—subject, verb, object, complement, modifier, and connector. Be sure the students understand the terms and the functions of each. Give them some class practice in separating subjects from verbs in their current reading. It is sometimes easier for them to find the essential skeleton of the sentence if they first cross out, or put in parentheses, all the prepositional phrases (which are usually modifiers, anyway). They can take these from their current reading—a textbook, the sports page, an advertisement, lyrics of a popular song, or the label on a ketchup bottle, or a soda can! This is an effective exercise because prepositional phrases are nearly always modifiers and almost never a part of the basic sentence. Then let them discuss the differences between phrases and clauses, between independent and dependent structures, between declarative and imperative sentences. Never assume that students will be adept at this kind of analysis. Guide them carefully with detailed explanations and many examples.

SUGGESTIONS FOR TEACHING CHAPTER 2—THE PATTERNS

CHAPTER 2, "The Twenty Patterns," is the heart of this book and contains enough material to keep your students busy throughout the semester as they incorporate the material into their compositions. Pace your discussions to fit your class; don't go faster than your students can master the techniques, and never try to cover more than three patterns in any one class period. Since there is a logical grouping and arrangement of the patterns, you may find it easier to go straight through from PATTERN 1 to PATTERN 20.

You will need to explain each of these patterns in great detail; you will also need to justify the rationale of the punctuation. Before you start with PATTERN 1, write some sentences on the board and review the sentence structure from CHAPTER 1.

Now, with your class, create appropriate graphic symbols to use when you analyze and discuss sentences. For example, you can use a double bar (‖) to separate subject and verb in independent clauses, or brackets to set off dependent clauses.

1. Draw one line under the main clause (in this case, the entire sentence):

    <u>The events of 9/11 ‖ exploded our old world and propelled us into a new era.</u>

2. Dramatize what happens when there are two independent clauses in the same sentence:

The events of 9/11 || shattered our old world (into smithereens); it || suddenly propelled us (into a completely new kind) (of world).

Draw a circle between the two independent clauses (which *could* be separate sentences); then explain that only four things can replace the circle:

a. a period, which would separate the clauses into two sentences;

b. a coordinating conjunction *(for, and, nor, but, or, yet, so)*—which can be remembered with the mnemonic FANBOYS—preceded by a comma;

c. a semicolon, sometimes followed by a connective such as *therefore* or *however*;

d. a colon, but *only if* the second clause explains or extends the idea of the first.

3. Use brackets to set off a dependent clause, and clarify its function as PART of the independent clause; use a single bar to separate the subject and the verb in the dependent clause:

   Marcie || bought [whatever she | wanted].

   (noun clause used as direct object)

   [What Tatum | needs] || is more discipline.

   (noun clause used as subject)

   The little children || played [where the fallen leaves | were deepest.]

   (dependent adverbial clause)

4. Use a wavy line under an absolute phrase:

   The war being over at last, the task (of arranging the peace terms) || began.

5. Use a circle around connectors and other nonfunctional terms.

   Next, it might be fun to show that these constructions work even with nonsense words. Provide one or two examples, and then let students put their own creations on the board and explain them.

   A bronsly sartian || swazzled (along the tentive clath).

   Yesterday I || thrombled (down the nat-fleuzed beach) [where glorphs and mizzles | lay (in the sun)].

After this review, the class should be ready to tackle the first group of sentence patterns—the compounds. Each of them is really just two sentences in one, but you must make clear the vast differences that are possible. Now is the time to have the class really master the Checkpoints under PATTERN 3, which cover the differences in the three compounds.

For exercises beyond those that accompany the pattern explanations, consider these ideas:

1. Follow your discussion of particular patterns by asking students to write ten sentences of their own using the patterns you assign. Have students label each sentence with the number of the pattern in the **left** margin. *The advantage of this book is the control you have through the pattern numbers.* For subject matter students can draw upon their reading, hobbies, sports, and other interests. If for any given assignment the entire class uses the same topic or idea, have the students compare how many different arrangements of words can express the same idea, but each with slightly different emphasis or rhythm.

2. Use SENTENCE PATTERN 1, the compound with a semicolon and without a conjunction, to teach or to test vocabulary. In the first clause of the compound sentence have students USE and UNDERLINE the given word; in the second clause have them DEFINE that word.

   EXAMPLE:

   > Zen Buddhism is an <u>esoteric</u> philosophy; only the initiated really understand it.

   OR THIS VARIATION:

   > The Greek root <u>chrono</u> means "time"; a chronometer measures time accurately. (See how much you can teach about punctuation in a sentence with this structure!)

3. Assign ten vocabulary words, each to be written in a different sentence pattern. Have students underline the vocabulary word and label the pattern by number in the left margin. When students give the pattern number of the structure they are imitating, you can check the accuracy of their understanding of the pattern at the same time you are checking the vocabulary word.

4. Require students to have at least one different pattern in each paragraph of their compositions. Have them write the number of the pattern they are imitating in the left margin. See "Marginalia: to encourage deliberate craftsmanship" (pp. xv–xvi) for more ways of encouraging students to analyze their writing as they improve their craftsmanship.

5. Have students collect interesting sentences from their reading and make a booklet of fifteen or twenty new and different patterns, with no more than two or three sentences plus analysis on each page. They may simply copy sentences they find, or they may clip and paste them

in their booklets, leaving room for a description (analysis) of each sentence in their own words.

6. Take a long, involved sentence from the assigned reading; have your students rewrite it several times using four or five different sentence patterns. (These revisions may have to contain some words that the original does not have.) Have students read these sentences aloud in class, commenting on the various effects thus achieved.

7. Point out the effectiveness of incorporating PATTERN 8 (the one with two or three dependent clauses) into a thesis or of using it to forecast main points in the introduction or to summarize in the conclusion.

8. Toward the end of the term, after they have mastered the patterns and know them by number, have students analyze some of their current reading, even from other courses. Have them write in the margin the numbers of the sentence patterns they find. (See CHAPTER 5 for two examples.)

9. Some of the example sentences for analysis are from professional writers; they are often convoluted and excessively detailed. Yet they can be springboards for discussion of such things as style, punctuation, sentence length, level and appropriateness of vocabulary, content, or even historical information.

10. At the end of the term, have the students compare their first attempts to their current efforts. They'll be surprised (and pleased) to see the improvement.

Suggestions for the Student

HOW TO GET THE MOST FROM THIS BOOK

The suggestions and exercises below may seem too simple or too artificial at first sight, but if you make a game of playing around with words, of fitting them to a formula, you will learn how to write sentences that have flair and variety, and that is a skill worth developing. A well-constructed sentence is, like any artful design, the result of sound craftsmanship; it actually involves and requires:

a. good composing or construction

b. appropriate punctuation

c. a feeling for the rhythm of language

d. an understanding of idiom

e. clarity of expression

f. recognition of the power of logical arrangement

If you are not in a composition class, but are working alone without a teacher's guidance, the suggestions below will help you to get the most out of this book, so follow them carefully. Don't be afraid to copy a pattern and fit your own words into it. Remember that every great craftsman begins as an apprentice imitating a master. By following the suggestions below and mastering the patterns, you will increase your skill in the art of styling sentences.

1. Study one pattern at a time. Write four or five sentences that follow that pattern exactly, especially the punctuation. Go through all twenty patterns in CHAPTER 2, taking only one at a time, until you are confident you understand the structure and the punctuation. Practice, practice—and more practice; this is the only way to learn.

2. In every paragraph you write, try to incorporate one or more of these patterns, especially when you find yourself tending to write short, simple sentences having the same kind of subject-verb structure. Keep trying to improve the quality and arrangement of all of your sentences, whether they follow one of these patterns or not.

3. Think of something you want to say and then practice writing it in three or four different ways, noticing the changes in effect and tone when you express the same idea with different patterns and punctuation. Since you may not be aware of these changes when you read silently, read aloud often to train your ear.

4. Analyze your reading material for eye-catching sentences, ones that you think have striking patterns you could imitate. (CHAPTER 5 shows you how.) Whether reading a newspaper, a magazine article, or a skillfully styled literary work, you will find many sentences so well written that you will want to analyze and then imitate them. Underline them; learn the pattern. Or from your reading make a collection of sentences that you have especially enjoyed. Or keep a special notebook of new and different patterns that you want to copy. In short, look for unusual and effective sentences in everything you read and make a conscious effort to add those new patterns to the basic twenty in CHAPTER 2.

5. Use your computer and its software to practice brainstorming and to capture ideas. Save your drafts on a disk, as they may be useful later. Practice using Spellcheck, Thesaurus, and other functions as you edit. The computer will help you plan, delete, add, and rearrange as you write and revise.

6. In early assignments, your instructor will probably be highly prescriptive. When you are told how many words, how many paragraphs, sometimes even how many sentences should occur within paragraphs, don't resent the detailed directions. Think about them as training in a skill. After all, athletic coaches and music instructors alike begin their training with strict regulations and drills, too. So follow all the "requirements."

MARGINALIA: TO ENCOURAGE DELIBERATE CRAFTSMANSHIP

ANALYSIS FOR THEMES

In every theme or paper you write there should be some goals, some design that you are trying to create. Marginalia can be a helpful guide for you, a way of checking up on what you are doing when you write. Marginalia, which, as the name implies, you write in the margin, will consist of words and symbols that indicate an analysis of your writing.

THINGS TO DO

1. Highlight the topic sentence of each paragraph. Identify it by the label **TS** in the margin.

2. In the **left** margin of each paragraph, indicate the attempted pattern from the sentence patterns (**SP**). Mark in the margin **SP 6** or **SP 9a**, for example.

3. Indicate a pronoun reference pattern in one of the paragraphs by drawing a circle around each pronoun and an arrow pointing to its antecedent. Identify in margin as **PRO PATT**.

4. Circle transitional words in one paragraph ("echo" words, transitional connectives, conjunctions).

5. List in the margin the types of sentences in one paragraph; use a variety of simple (**S**), complex (**CX**), compound (**C**), and compound complex (**CCX**).

6. When you master a new vocabulary word, underline it and label it **VOC**.

You might want to use a different color for each type of entry so that you can see at a glance whether you have incorporated all the techniques of good construction. These marks might seem distracting at first, but the results will be worth the distraction. A glance at the marginalia will indicate whether you understand the composition techniques being taught.

Why bother with all of this? Because it works. There is no better answer. You will come to realize that a theme must have a variety of sentences, that there must be transitional terms if the theme is to have coherence, that pronouns help eliminate needless repetition of the same word, that synonyms and figurative language give the theme more sparkle than you ever hoped for. Your instructors will like what they are reading; you will like what you are writing, and your grades will improve.

The following pages show two paragraphs written by a student. Note the marginal analysis and the effectiveness of the different sentence patterns.

A PARAGRAPH ANALYZING
A SIMILE IN POETRY

THE MOVEMENT OF TIME

MARGINALIA

"Like as the waves make towards the pebbled shore,
So do our minutes hasten to their end. . . ."

—*William Shakespeare*, SONNET LX

TS

    In the first two lines of Sonnet LX, Shakespeare uses a simile comparing the waves of the ocean to the minutes of our life: "Like as the waves make towards the pebbled shore, / So do our minutes hasten to their

SP3
SP11

end. . . ." This line is inverted: that is, the subject "our minutes" is in the second line, and the comparison "like as the waves" is in the first line. The simile says, in effect, that "the minutes of our lives are like the waves on the shore." The waves roll end-

VOC≠SP1

lessly, <u>inexorably</u> toward the shore of the ocean; the minutes of our lives hasten endlessly toward the end of our lives. This figure of speech gives an image of movement. We can almost see time, like ocean waves,

SP10
SP16

moving toward its destiny: the end of life. Just as the waves end on the shore, so too our life's minutes end in death. Some words in the simile have particular

SP3≠VOC
a repeated SVO
pattern

power: the word hasten <u>conjures</u> up a mental picture of rapid movement, of inexorable hurry toward some predestined end. The word towards suggests a straight, unerring path going without hesitation or pause to some goal. The waves move toward their

repeated SP10

goal: the shore. Our minutes move toward their goal: life's end. This simile is a very effective, picture-

PRO PATT
SP9
Repeat of keyword

making figure of speech. (It) paints a mental picture of movement and destiny. (It) suggests a very important (fact) about life, a fact we must remember. That (fact) is the truth expressed here beautifully by Shakespeare—life goes on forever toward its end,

Summary of TS
with "echo" of quote

never slowing down or going back. Our lives do indeed "hasten to their end."

—Shawn Waddell

A PARAGRAPH DEFINING A TERM

MARGINALIA

A JUNK-MAN

TS
Order: general
to Particular
SP4A

SP14
SP12

VOC

Metaphor

VOC
SP1

Contrast
SP9
Definition of TS
repeated word
for coherence

Example

factual data

Contrast
VOC and two
levels of diction
SP1
echo of TS
for coherence

A junk-man in baseball is the most feared pitcher of all. Most batters go to the plate with the knowledge that the pitcher usually throws either curves or fastballs or knuckleballs in the clinch. From his view at the plate, a batter sees a curveball pitcher's curve starting off in a line seemingly headed straight for his head. Fortunately, just before making any painful contact, the ball seems to change its own mind, veering away to the opposite side of the plate. But after long and <u>arduous</u> practice, any batter can learn to anticipate or recognize a curve and be prepared for it. The same is true for a fastball that blurs its way into the catcher's mitt or for a knuckleball which seems to have trouble deciding where to go. A veteran batter can learn to sense the sometimes <u>erratic</u> path of either ball; he can feel some confidence when he has some idea of the pitcher's preferred ball. But he can be put completely off stride when he hears he has to face that most dreaded of all pitchers, a junk-man—dreaded because he can throw all pitches with equal effectiveness and surprise. This element of surprise coupled with variety makes the junk-man the most feared of all pitchers in baseball. For example, when Sam the Slugger goes to bat, he can feel more relaxed if he knows that Carl the Curve-man will probably throw curves about seventy-five percent of the time. The same is true for Sam when a well-known fastballer or knuckler is facing him from sixty feet away. On the contrary, Sam the Slugger loses his <u>equanimity</u> and is tied in knots when Joe the Junk-man grins wickedly across that short sixty feet from mound to plate; Sam has no way to anticipate what surprises may lurk behind that wicked grin when he faces the most feared pitcher in baseball.

—Shawn Waddell

CHAPTER 1

The Sentence

WHAT EXACTLY IS A SENTENCE?

Like sign language, the beat of drums, or smoke signals, a sentence is a means of communicating. A sentence expresses a complete thought and contains at least one subject-verb combination. It may express emotions, give orders, make statements, or ask questions. In every case, sentences are meant to communicate.

Sometimes, a sentence may be a single word:

What?   Nonsense!   Jump.

"What?" and "Nonsense!" communicate a complete thought. "Jump," though, has an unspoken "you" as the subject.

Most sentences, however, have two parts: the subject, which is a noun or pronoun, and the verb. These two parts follow a basic pattern:

<u>Subject</u> || <u>Verb</u>

Let's break up some very simple sentences into their two parts, using vertical lines to separate the different parts.

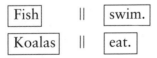

Make up your own examples, following the pattern above; box the subject and the verb, and put a pair of vertical lines (||) between these two basic sentence parts. You need only the S (subject) slot and the V (verb) slot.

To be more expressive, you can add some descriptive words (called modifiers) to the subject, the verb, or both. You still have two slots and need only one pair of vertical lines:

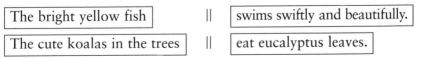

By combining the S slot and the V slot, you can construct the most common sentence patterns. Each sentence has a name that describes its purpose and what it does:

NAME	TASK
DECLARATIVE	A sentence may make a statement.
INTERROGATIVE	May it also ask a question?
IMPERATIVE	Use it to give an order.
EXCLAMATORY	What great emotion it can express!

The subject-verb combination will be the heart of each sentence you write. It will let you build an amazing variety of sentence patterns. Even long sentences may have only one pair of vertical lines.

When you add descriptive words, the sentences get longer. Some sentences have *phrases*—a group of words that have no subject-verb combination and usually act as a modifier. There are several kinds of phrases:

PREPOSITIONAL PHRASE	begins with a preposition (*in, on, at, under,* and so on) (for example, *in* the park, *on* the table, *over* the door)
PARTICIPIAL PHRASE	begins with a present or past participle (for example, *leading* the pack, *grown* in the summer)
INFINITIVE PHRASE	begins with an infinitive (*to* plus the verb) (for example, *to play* tennis, *to stop* the project)

You might also expand a basic sentence with *clauses*—a group of words containing a subject-verb combination that can express a complete thought, but may not:

INDEPENDENT CLAUSE	makes a complete statement communicates an idea by itself
DEPENDENT CLAUSE	modifies part of another clause does not communicate a complete thought may be a part of another clause

Independent clauses and dependent clauses can be combined to form various types of sentences. The most common types of sentences are:

SIMPLE	makes a single statement is an independent clause has only one subject-verb combination

COMPOUND	makes two or more statements
	has two or more independent clauses
	has two or more subject-verb combinations
COMPLEX	has an independent clause
	has one or more dependent clauses functioning as modifiers
COMPOUND COMPLEX	has two or more independent clauses
	has two or more subject-verb combinations
	has one or more dependent clauses functioning as modifiers

Sometimes there will be only *one* subject; sometimes there will be *two or more* subjects in the S slot but they will come before the ‖ lines. The V, too, may have one or more verbs. As you analyze sentences, note that each subject-verb combination will require a new pair of vertical lines.

<u>John</u> and <u>David</u> ‖ <u>raced</u> cars but <u>drove</u> safely.

NOTE: Throughout the book, one line indicates the <u>subject</u>; two lines indicate the <u>verb</u>.

Sentences can have something extra, but still have one pair of vertical lines. With transitive verbs (verbs that describe an action the subject performs) you need a direct object (DO). A DO receives the action of the verb and answers the questions "What?" or "Whom?"

EXAMPLES:

DO
<u>Jason</u> ‖ <u>lost</u> his skateboard.

DO   **DO**
<u>Tamara</u> ‖ <u>forgot</u> her books but <u>passed</u> the test.

Certain verbs, listed below, are linking verbs and may have a subject complement—a noun, pronoun, or adjective—that renames or describes the subject:

Being verbs	am, are, is, was, were, be, being, been
Verbs of sensation	feel, taste, etc.
Other linking verbs	appear, become, seem

The following sentences illustrate the S-V combination with one or more subject complements.

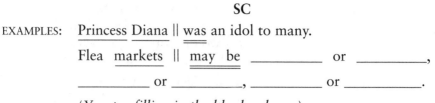

SC

EXAMPLES: Princess Diana ‖ was an idol to many.

Flea markets ‖ may be _____ or _____,

_____ or _____, _____ or _____.

(*You try filling in the blanks above.*)

You can add modifying words to almost any part of the sentence and phrases. You can keep the single subject-verb combination or else expand your sentence to include several subject-verb combinations, all having modifiers. Mark main clauses by putting ‖ between the S and the V in a main clause and | between the S and the V in dependent clauses; then put brackets around dependent clauses.

EXAMPLES:

Long or short sentences ‖ can sometimes communicate effectively the most difficult ideas in the world. (simple)

Sterling silver [that ‖ may cost $800 a place setting] and small kitchen appliances like can openers or toasters [that | are considered too basic] ‖ are no longer popular wedding gifts. (complex)

Now let's break a whole sentence into its parts. When making a mechanical analysis of any sentence, use the following labels to identify the various parts:

S	subject	**C**	connector (conjunction)	**M**	modifier
V	verb	**O**	object of preposition	**IO**	indirect object
			object of infinitive	**OC**	object complement
SC	subject complement	**P**	preposition	**DO**	direct object

NOTE: For further explanation of these terms, see one of the reference books listed at the end of this chapter.

The following sentence illustrates the type of analysis you might practice:

M   M   M   S   V   M   SC   P M

The rundown, dirty shoes appeared unbelievably incongruous on the

O

model.

The following chapters will help you write more effective sentences and will give you clues to spice up your writing. Sentences come to life as a writer plans them; in fact, very few fine sentences are spontaneous. The following pages give you models to imitate and use. These basic patterns are by no means the only ones. As your writing matures, you will discover additional patterns. As you master the ability to analyze and to compose sentences, you will be justifiably proud of your improving style.

And now you're off . . . on the way to creating better sentences and more polished paragraphs.

SOME HELPFUL REFERENCES

For detailed information, materials, and examples of sentences, you may wish to consult one of the following recent publications:

Bizzell, Patricia et al. *The Bedford Bibliography for Teachers of Writing.* 3rd ed. Boston: St. Martin's, 1996 (free to instructors).

Diamond, Harriet, and Phyllis Dutwin. *Grammar in Plain English.* Hauppauge, NY: Barron's Educational Series, 1997.

Hacker, Diana. *A Writer's Reference,* 4th ed. Boston: St. Martin's, 1999.

Hairston, Maxine. *The Scott, Foresman Handbook for Writers.* 6th ed. New York: Longman, 2001.

Kolln, Martha. *Rhetorical Grammar: Grammatical Choices, Rhetorical Effects.* 3rd ed. Needham Heights, MA: Allyn & Bacon, 1998.

——. *Understanding English Grammar.* 6th ed. New York: Longman, 2001.

Reid, Stephen. *The Prentice Hall Handbook for College Writers.* 5th ed. Englewood Cliffs, NJ: Prentice Hall, 1999.

Skwire, David, and Harvey S. Wiener. *Student's Book of College English,* 9th ed. New York: Longman, 2001.

Troyka, Lynn Quitman. *Simon & Schuster Handbook for Writers,* 6th ed. Upper Saddle River, NJ: Prentice Hall, 2002.

CHAPTER 2

The Twenty Patterns

NOW LET'S MAKE SENTENCES GROW . . .

This chapter introduces you to the twenty basic patterns that writers use to add style and variety. These patterns will not be new to you; you've already seen them many times in things you've read. Probably you never thought about analyzing the patterns or realized that they could help you perk up your own writing.

Study them. Give them a chance to help you.

COMPOUND CONSTRUCTIONS

In CHAPTER 1 we covered the simplest kinds of sentences. The easiest way to expand this basic pattern is to join two simple sentences to make a compound sentence.

PATTERN 1:   COMPOUND SENTENCE: SEMICOLON,
NO CONJUNCTION
(two short, related sentences now joined)

S   V   ;   S   V   .

Explanation

This pattern helps you join two short, simple sentences having two closely related ideas. They need a semicolon instead of a conjunction and comma. The illustration in the box and the examples show only two clauses; you can actually have three or more. Be sure to avoid two pitfalls of the compound sentence:

1. The fused or run-on sentence (which has no punctuation between the two sentences that have been joined).
    EXAMPLE: My cat lost her ball I don't know where.
2. The comma splice (using a comma instead of a period, semicolon, or colon to separate the two sentences you have joined).
    EXAMPLE: The plant wilted, I forgot to water it.

You avoid the above two problems if you faithfully copy the following patterns for compound sentences, being careful to imitate the punctuation exactly.

Remember that an independent clause has a subject-verb combination that makes a full statement. What precedes and what follows the semicolon (PATTERN 1) must be capable of standing alone; otherwise, it is only a fragment.

This is a fragment:

At the game, the reason for the loss in yardage being
the broken shoestring on the left guard's shoe.

Being is the wrong verb form; change it to *was* and the phrase becomes a complete thought—and a sentence.

This is another kind of fragment:

Which was the only explanation that he could give at that moment.

This fragment is a dependent clause, even though it has the subject-verb combinations *which* and *he could give*. It is not a complete sentence because it begins with the subordinating word *which*. Change *which* to *it* and you now have a complete thought.

Subordinating words, such as the following, keep a clause from being independent:

because
if
when
after
and other such sub-
ordinating words

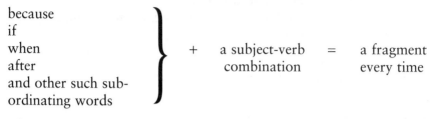

+   a subject-verb   =   a fragment
     combination   every time

These are some common semicolon errors:

Because so many of us work 24/7; . . .
The dance having started at 8:30; . . .
For example; . . .

These three errors can be easily corrected in this way:

For example, . . . (*Use a comma instead of a semicolon.*)

Because so many of us work 24/7, we are often cranky. (*Finish the idea to make a complete sentence.*)

The dance started at 8:30. (*Use the correct form of the verb to make a complete sentence.*)

NOTE: Be careful to not confuse commas and semicolons.

WHEN TO USE THIS PATTERN

Use this pattern when you have talked about similar ideas in several sentences. If you combine these ideas, you will have a single, more powerful sentence. When revising, look for paragraphs with many short sentences that have parallel ideas and ask yourself, "Can I combine these sentences to give my message a more forceful impact?"

Examples

Gloria, try on these jeans; they seem to be your size.

Some people dream of being something; others stay awake and are.

Reading is the easy part; remembering takes more effort.

Professional examples

We've included some professional examples for analysis. Study these examples to see how experienced writers handle the various patterns. See how they manipulate word order and punctuation to get their message across and create interest through sentence variety. Don't be afraid to imitate, praise, or criticize these examples.

"He who knows others is wise; he who knows himself is enlightened."—Lao-tzu

"Singapore has 11,910 people per square mile; Mongolia has only three." —*Condé Nast Traveler*

"My forefathers didn't come over on the Mayflower; they met the boat."—Will Rogers

"Sign up for our Family Plan and you can share minutes with our one-rate plan; if you sign up now, you can take advantage of our special rate."—Ad for Nokia

"It made no sense to anyone; it was just style."—*SF Chronicle*

Variations

Once you're comfortable with PATTERN 1, you can start varying it in some interesting ways.

PATTERN 1A

The first variation, PATTERN 1a, uses a conjunctive adverb (connector) such as *however, hence, therefore, thus, then, moreover, nevertheless, likewise, consequently,* and *accordingly.*

You still need a semicolon *before* the connector, but a comma *after* the connector is optional.

<u>   S   V   </u> ; however, <u>   S   V   </u> .

EXAMPLES: She exercised every day and cut back on her food; however, she didn't lose any weight.

This car looks as if it has been wrecked; therefore it's not a good buy.

PATTERN 1B

For the second variation, PATTERN 1b, use one of the coordinating conjunctions (also connectors): *for, and, nor, but, or, yet,* or *so.* You can remember them easily by their first letters and call them FANBOYS.

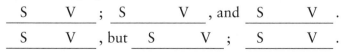

<u>   S   V   </u> ; <u> S   V </u> , and <u> S   V </u> .

<u>   S   V   </u> , but <u> S   V </u> ; <u> S   V </u> .

EXAMPLES: The rain kept falling; Joan saw the roof begin to leak, and she put out a bucket to catch the water.

It was the right color; it fit, and it was cheap.

Our cat loves to play with the ball; I love to watch her, but sometimes I'm not in the mood to play.

I didn't do it; John said he didn't do it, but the vase was certainly broken.

PATTERN 1C

In this third variation, PATTERN 1c, use two or more semicolons to connect three or more complete sentences:

$$\underline{\text{S}\quad\text{V}}\ ;\ \underline{\text{S}\quad\text{V}}\ ;\ \underline{\text{S}\quad\text{V}}\ .$$

EXAMPLES: John got an A; Jennie also got an A; unfortunately George got a C.

Carmen likes to cook; Janice would rather watch TV; I like to eat Carmen's cooking and watch TV with Janice.

Dad is a skinflint; when I ask for a loan, he doesn't listen; Mom isn't any help either.

Exercises

To give you some practice with PATTERN 1, complete each of the following sentences with an independent clause:

1. _____

the beach was deserted and rather scary.

2. After they lost the match, the tennis team went home;

_____.

3. The large blue whale came very close to the boat; _____.

Complete each of the following sentences by adding an appropriate conjunctive adverb (PATTERN 1a):

1. I really didn't want to go to the party; _____ I went to be with Jim.

2. My teacher has traveled extensively; _____ I asked her advice about Italy.

3. I have to feed the pets when I get home; _____ I have to have supper started by the time Mom gets home.

Combine the short sentences into one sentence that follows PATTERN 1b. If necessary, add, omit, or change words to improve the sentence.

GROUP ONE: The girl looks happy.
              She has a new car.
              Her brother has one too.

_____

_____

GROUP TWO: The tiger seems restless.
              He is really big.
              He should have more room.

_____

_____

GROUP THREE: Fettuccini is a delicious pasta.
              It is a favorite dish in many European countries.
              It is often associated with Italy.
              A person who likes fettuccini is not always Italian.

_____

_____

When you read, watch for sentences that follow these patterns. List some you find here:

_____

_____

_____

_____

_____

_____

_____

_____

```
PATTERN 2:      COMPOUND SENTENCE WITH
                ELLIPTICAL CONSTRUCTION
                (comma indicates the omitted verb)
                              (omitted verb)
 S    V    DO  or  SC ;  S         ,        DO   or    SC .
```

Explanation

This pattern echoes PATTERN 1, but we leave out the verb in the second clause BECAUSE and ONLY IF it would needlessly repeat the verb of the first clause. Notice also, you may have a direct object (DO), which receives the action of the verb; or you may have a subject complement (SC), which describes the subject. The comma says to the reader, "Mentally insert the same verb you have already read in the first clause."

You need parallel wording in both clauses, and the verb must be exactly the same.

For example, this is not parallel:

We (S)   like (V)   classical   music (DO)   ;

George   ,   punk   rock (DO)   .

The reader can't use the verb from the first clause and put it where the comma is, because "George like punk rock" is ungrammatical. The correct form is, "George likes punk rock." Sometimes the verb is exactly like the one in the first clause, but you may still have an awkward-sounding sentence if you omit too many words or if you forget the importance of rhythm and sound.

To see how this works, read this aloud:

Bill played a musical number by Bach; Joan, Beethoven.

This sentence sounds as if Bill played something written by three people!

Now read this aloud:

Bill played a musical number by Bach; Joan, one by Beethoven.

When you leave out more than the verb, you may need to put in a word, such as *one* here. The sentence above and the one below leave out more than just the verb; you might even leave out the subject *and* the verb:

An artist's instinct is intuitive, not rational; aesthetic, not pragmatic.

WHEN TO USE THIS PATTERN

This pattern may look easy but it is actually very sophisticated. Still, when you don't want to repeat the same verb in the second or third clause, this pattern can be helpful. You'll have to develop your ear to test whether it's the right time for PATTERN 2. Does the sentence sound natural and have a rhythmical balance? If it is awkward or unclear, it is not the right time to use this pattern.

Examples

The mother and son each had a goal; hers, educational; his, recreational.

For many of us, the new math teacher was a savior; for others, a pain.

His mother told him to rent a car; his sister, to pack the suitcases.

Professional examples

"Thought is the blossom; language [,] the bud; action [,] the fruit."—Ralph Waldo Emerson

NOTE: The brackets indicate that the commas do not appear in the original sentence.

"Lou Williams was in for adultery; John Jones for gambling."—*Wall Street Journal*, 7/16/01

Checkpoints

✓ Be sure that each sentence really has two independent clauses in it, even though the second one has an unexpressed verb or other words.

✓ Be sure that the verb omitted in the second clause matches exactly, in form and tense, the verb in the first clause.

✓ After the semicolon, if more than the verb is left out, be sure the structure is still parallel and the thought complete.

✓ Use a semicolon if there is no conjunction; if there is a conjunction (one of the FANBOYS mentioned in PATTERN 1), many writers use a comma. A semicolon NEVER goes with a coordinating conjunction.

Exercises

To practice what you've learned, complete the following sentences. (1) If the first clause is missing, fill in a complete clause (with a verb) so it makes sense. (2) If the second clause is missing, fill in the blank leaving out the verb and whatever else might be just repetition.

Examples

The *painting on the wall represents chaos to Fred*; to Alice, a wonderland.

or

The dove is the universal symbol for peace; *the hawk, for war*.

1. Going to carnivals makes me happy;

   _____ .

2. _____ ;

   violent movies, uncomfortable.

3. _____ ; Ireland and Scotland, much greener.

4. All the children want to go to McDonald's for lunch; _____

   _____ .

As you read, notice sentences that follow this pattern and add them below.

_____

_____

_____

_____

_____

_____

_____

_____

_____

_____

> **PATTERN 3:**   COMPOUND SENTENCE WITH
>   EXPLANATORY STATEMENT
>   (clauses separated by a colon)
>
> General statement (idea) : specific statement (example).
>
> (an independent clause)   (an independent clause)

Explanation

This pattern is exactly like PATTERNS 1 and 2 in structure: Although it is a compound, it is very different in content, as the colon implies. The colon performs a special function: It signals the reader that something important or explanatory will follow (as this very sentence illustrates). In this particular pattern, the colon signals that the second clause will specifically explain or expand some idea expressed only vaguely in the first clause.

The first statement will contain a word or an idea that needs explaining; the second statement will give some specific information or example about that idea.

WHEN TO USE THIS PATTERN

Use it when you want the second part of a sentence to explain the first part, give an example, or provide an answer to an implied question.

In the following examples, notice that the first independent statement mentions something in a general way: "a harsh truth," "a single horrifying meaning." Then the independent statement after the colon answers the questions: "What harsh truth?" "Which horrifying meaning?" The second clause makes the first one clear.

Examples

Darwin's *The Origin of Species* forcibly states a harsh truth: Only the fittest survive.

The empty coffin in the center of the crypt had a single horrifying meaning: Dracula had left his tomb to stalk the village streets in search of fresh blood.

Remember Yogi Berra's advice: It ain't over till it's over.

NOTE: Some writers capitalize the first word after the colon in this pattern, but this is a matter of personal taste and styling.

A lizard never worries about losing its tail: It can always grow another.

"Weekdays are very similar to identical suitcases: They are all the same size, but some people can pack more into them than others."—Joel Gutierrez

All agreed she was well qualified: She graduated from Harvard with a 4.0 grade point average.

Superman has extraordinary powers: He flies like a bird and has X-ray vision.

Professional examples

"The murmuring water, the morning fresh garden unheated yet by the lemon sun, the flight of a white-browed blackbird: all helped to make unreal the tableau of the man kneeling by the sundial."—Reginald Hill, *Ruling Passion*

"One thing you learn when you love the Red Sox like I do: how to lose and get up and fight another day."—Jack Welch (CEO at G.E.)

"Such disputes are occasionally satisfying: you can take pleasure in knowing you have converted someone to your point of view."—Alfred Rosa and Paul Eschholz, *Models for Writers*

"Old cars and young children have several things in common: Both are a responsibility and have to be fed often or they break down."—Claudia Glenn Downing, *Lear's*, November 1992

NOTE: The sentence above has a capital letter after the colon and a final clause beginning with the coordinator *or*. The final clause is so short that the author chose to omit the comma before the coordinator.

Checkpoints

✓ Now that you have learned all three of the compound constructions, notice the differences among them. PATTERNS 1, 2, and 3 are NOT simply three different ways to punctuate the same sentence. The words must perform different functions; the sentences must do different things:

PATTERN 1 must make two closely related statements about the same idea, statements you do not want to punctuate as two separate sentences;

PATTERN 2 must have a specific word or words from the first clause implied but not stated in the second—otherwise no ellipsis is possible;

PATTERN 3 must have a second independent clause that in some way amplifies or explains the idea stated in the first independent clause. Do not use this pattern with a colon unless the second statement is related to the first.

✓ Remember the test for every compound sentence: both clauses must be full statements and capable of standing alone as sentences.

Exercises

Complete each of the following sentences with an independent clause. (1) If the first clause is missing, provide a general statement. (2) If the second clause is missing, add an explanation.

1. _____ :

   the students all got A's on their papers.

2. The dot-com companies have changed the work week: _____

   _____ .

3. I finally know how to program my VCR: _____

   _____ .

4. The reporter asked her the most important question: _____

   _____ .

5. _____ :

   we toured the National Air and Space Museum, the Smithsonian Castle, the Freer Gallery, and the new wing of the National Gallery of Art.

As you read, watch for sentences that follow this pattern and add them below.

_____

_____

_____

_____

_____

_____

_____

SENTENCES WITH SERIES

PATTERNS 4–8, which follow, all use series in sentences in a variety of ways.

WHAT IS A SERIES?

When you see or hear the word *series,* what comes immediately to mind? The World Series? A bowling series? A television series? Let's think about how the word *series* applies to sentence structure.

A series is a group of three or more similar items, which all go in the same slot of the sentence. All items in the series must be similar in form (for example, all nouns or all verbs) because they have the same grammatical function. You may have a series in any slot of the sentence: three or four verbs for the same subject; three or four objects for the same preposition; three or four nouns or adjectives in the object or complement slot. You may have a series with any part of speech, not only with single words but also with phrases or dependent clauses. You may also arrange the items in different patterns:

A, B, C	A and B and C	A, B, and C

or with paired items:

A and B   ,   C and D   ,   E and F

WHEN IS A SERIES HELPFUL?

A series can help eliminate wordiness. If, for example, you have three short sentences, you can reduce them to a single sentence with a series. If you want to list or give several examples, try series structures to provide details. For variety, you might create this pattern without the conjunction, to give a different kind of emphasis to the items of the series. You do not single out the last item for special emphasis; instead, you say that all the items are equal.

PATTERN 4:   A SERIES WITHOUT A CONJUNCTION
(a series in any place in the sentence)

A, B, C _____ .

Explanation

This pattern is the simplest form of the series. You just separate the items by commas. No conjunction links the final two items. Omitting this conjunction is effective because it gives your sentence a quick, staccato sound.

Read the series aloud so you can hear whether the items flow together *without* the conjunction before the last item. Remember that tone and sound and fluency are important here. Also, remember that each item should receive equal emphasis.

Develop your ear!

Examples

The United States has a government of the people, by the people, for the people.

The teacher handled the situation with great patience, wisdom, humor.

It took courage, skill, knowledge—and he had them all.

Their friendship has endured, in spite of arguments, boyfriends, distance.

I like big burgers with everything on 'em: pickles, onions, tomato, lettuce, plenty of mustard.

Professional examples

"I have come to you without sin, without guile, without evil, without a witness against me."—*The Book of the Dead*

"They focus on the bottom line, and through their knowledge make decisions about which projects and products to fund, which to cut, which strategies will work, which will not."—*LineZine*, September 2001

"One group will respond to wit, another to Biblical quotations, still another to a spread of statistics."—*The Language of Argument*

"Whether 60 or 16, there is in every human being's heart the love of wonder, the sweet amazement of the stars and the starlike things, the undaunted challenge of events, the unfailing childlike appetite of 'what-next' in the joy of the game of living."—Stanley Ullman, fifteenth-century French essayist

"Do you often feel dragged out, knocked down, pooped, bushed—plumb exhausted?"—*MM* Magazine, December 2001

Sentences for analysis

Look carefully at the following series patterns. Do you get lost as you read them? Is there too much detail?

1. Do you see ways of breaking up this overlong sentence into two or more shorter ones that are not overwhelming? Or do you think the sentence is effective stylistically?

   "Robert Mondavi's father, Cesare, came from Sassafarento near Ancona, on the Adriatic coast of the Marches—not a particularly rich or fertile part of Italy even now, nor, except for Verdicchio, much of a wine-growing region, and a good deal less so, no doubt, in 1883, when Cesare was born, the son of a large, simple family and possibly the first member of it, I have read somewhere, to be able to sign his name."—Cyril Ray, "Robert Mondavi of the Napa Valley"

   _____

   _____

2. The following sentence has a lengthy series joined by repeated possessive pronouns. Do you think the sentence is effective or weak? What feature contributes strength or detracts from the rhetorical effectiveness?

   "Walled off from the roaring traffic of the Embankment and Fleet Street and High Holborn, each Inn is a self-centered community with its own gardens, lush with cherry and magnolia, camelia, and crocus; its own library; its own dining hall; its labyrinth of walks and lawns; its blocks of offices and flats let out mostly to barristers."—Robert Wernick, *Smithsonian*, May 1992

   _____

   _____

3. Watch how Kathryn Marshall combines a number of rhetorical strategies with her series structures. She alludes to Bugsy Siegel and the founding of Las Vegas, she underscores her emotion by repeating the word *ever,* and she creates a number of images with her various verb choices suggesting the movement of light.

"In my room, I stood at the darkened window and looked out at the neo-wonderland. The lights rippled, rolled, darted, sequenced their way through fantastical patterns against the black, empty screen of beyond, millions and millions of lights, more than crazy Bugsy could have imagined, far more than someone who's never spent a night in Las Vegas could ever, ever, ever—even in the wildest reaches of dreams—hope to comprehend."—Kathryn Marshall, *American Way,* September 1991

_____

_____

Checkpoint

✓ Since any part of the sentence may have a series, take care to make all items in the series parallel in form as they are already parallel in function.

These sentences are not parallel so they are awkward:

The typical teenage user of snuff is white, active, and athletic, and subjected to very heavy peer pressure.

Swimming, surfing, to go boating—these were Sally's favorite sports at the summer camp.

Now explain why these revisions are better:

The typical teenage user of snuff is white, active, athletic, and peer pressure is very heavy.

Swimming, surfing, boating—these were Sally's favorite sports at the summer camp.

NOTE: Although in this book we do not discuss the most common pattern for series—A, B, and C—remember that a comma before the conjunction often helps make the meaning clear.

Shakespeare uses an image, a metaphor, a simile and rhyme scheme to clarify his theme in this sonnet. (A "simile and rhyme" scheme? Without the comma before the conjunction, that's what the sentence says!)

The restaurant served four varieties of sandwiches: corned beef, pastrami, salami and egg with bacon. (Would you order the last one?)

NOTE: Some style manuals omit the comma before the conjunction and the last item unless it is needed for clarity.

Exercises

Develop a series for each of the following sentences.

1. An essay traditionally has three major parts:

   ———————————————— , ———————————————— ,

   ———————————————— .

2. ———————————————— , ———————————————— ,

   ———————————————— are my favorite foods.

3. (Begin this sentence with three *-ed* or *-en* words.)

   ———————————————— , ———————————————— ,

   ———————————————— , the winner left the stadium feeling

   great.

4. (Provide a series of *-ing* words for the blanks.) The children gathered around their teacher, ———————————————— ,

   ———————————————— , ———————————————— .

5. When the game was cancelled, the rowdy spectators at the ball game

   ———————————————— , ———————————————— ,

   ———————————————— .

As you read, watch for sentences that follow this pattern and add them below.

———————————————————————————————

———————————————————————————————

———————————————————————————————

———————————————————————————————

———————————————————————————————

———————————————————————————————

———————————————————————————————

PATTERN 4a: A SERIES WITH A VARIATION

A or B or C   .   (in any place in the sentence)

A and B and C   .   (in any place in the sentence)

Explanation

You may want to vary the preceding pattern at times and write a series with conjunctions between all items (but usually not more than three). Again, let your ear be your guide. Listen for the tumbling rhythm in the following sentences.

Examples

Looking down from the Empire State Building, Jeannie felt thrilled and amazed—and scared.

Even though he is smart, I have never seen Keith arrogant or annoyed or impatient.

Many ice hockey games lead to broken ribs or sprained knees or dislocated shoulders—or even worse.

Collies and geese and children tumbled out of the farmhouses in Alsace Lorraine, barking or hissing or shouting according to their unique French natures.

The intense heat and the exhaustion and the twenty-six miles had confused and crippled Gabriela Scheiss, but there was something in her spirit that sustained her during the 1988 Los Angeles Olympic marathon.

Professional examples

"During World War II from fall into the summer of 1940, Germany rolled into Poland and Denmark and Norway and Holland and Belgium and finally France."—Fred Strebeigh, *Smithsonian*

(Do you think a dash before the final *and* would have made the sentence more dramatic?)

"As long as rivers shall run down to the sea, or shadows touch the mountains, or stars graze in the vault of heaven, so long shall your honor, your name, your praises endure."—Virgil, *Ecologies*

NOTE: The sentence above uses PATTERN 4a for the first series and PATTERN 4 in the second series.

"When I'm crying over a story like that or I'm frustrated or unhappy, my housekeeper will say, 'Now it's all right; we'll have a cup of tea.' "—Oprah Winfrey

Sentences for analysis

Not all writers are fully in control of their style. Often you'll find long sentences in your reading piled so full of information that you lose the train of the author's thought.

1. Below Clark Kimball overloads his sentence with printing vocabulary. Since Kimball is lecturing, is this long sentence more—or less—of a problem than if he were writing? Is the sentence successful, or do you have trouble remembering earlier parts by the time you reach the end? How might you break up the sentence into two or three shorter ones?

   "The paper, the ink, the letter forms—the Romans, the italics, the serifs and sans serifs—the ligatures, impressions, spacing, leading, margin, gutter; the plates, illustrations, frontispieces, head and tail pieces; colophons; borders, rules, folios, ding-bats; title pages, half-titles; cloths, papers, boards; stampings, debossings, labels, bands, cases—these are some of the words of the typographer—challenging and magic words—each laden and potent with meaning—each of which must be put at the service of the subject matter, and simultaneously in harmony with each other!"—Clark Kimball, Carl Hertzog Lecture Series, *The Southwest Printer*, 1990

   _____

   _____

2. Analyze the following sentence for its length, detail, punctuation, and clarity. How could it be made clearer?

   "Sir Thomas More and Sir Francis Drake and Sir Walter Raleigh and Shakespeare's Sir John Falstaff, Sir Francis Bacon and John Donne, Sir William Blackstone and William Penn and William Pitt, Boswell and Fielding and Sheridan and De Quincy and Lamb and Thackeray and

Macaulay, King Edward VII, Margaret Thatcher, and of course, Rumpole of the Bailey—all took their meals at an Inn of Court."— Henry Wiencek, *Smithsonian*, May 1992

_____

_____

3. Here is another series that loses readers. How could you eliminate some of the clumsiness? What makes the sentence so forbidding?

"The Prado offers as breathtaking a panorama of soaring peaks like Velazquez and Francisco Goya and Hieronymus Bosch and El Greco and Titian and Bartolome Esteban Murillo and Jose Ribera and Peter Paul Rubens and Sandro Botticelli, with stretches of flatland or desert in between."—Stanley Meisler, "Spain's Prado," *Smithsonian*, January 1992

_____

_____

Exercises

For each of the following incomplete sentences create a series with conjunctions, omitting commas.

1. When I walked on the beach, I felt the afternoon sun had tinted it

_____ and _____

and _____ .

2. The best programs on TV now are _____

and _____

and _____ .

3. _____ and _____

_____ and _____

seem to be issues for many students.

4. The science conference board couldn't decide whether to concentrate

on _____

or _____ or _____ .

5. All that is _____ or _____

_____ or _____ or

_____ seems to be harmful to one's health.

Write sentences using the series listed below. For one group use no conjunctions between the items; in another add a conjunction between them.

1. oranges   peaches   kiwis   mangoes

_____

_____

_____

2. soccer in spring   baseball in summer
    hockey in winter   football in the fall

_____

_____

_____

3. red beans   green beans   garbanzo beans

_____

_____

_____

As you read, watch for sentences that follow this pattern and add them below.

_____

_____

_____

_____

_____

_____

_____

_____

_____

PATTERN 5:	A SERIES OF BALANCED PAIRS (note the rhythm)

A and B   ,   C and D   ,   E and F   .

(may be in any slot in the sentence)

Explanation

This pattern has a series of pairs—two or three or four, with a conjunction between the items in each pair. This construction creates a balanced rhythm, but how can you tell if this rhythm is right for your sentence? Read the sentence aloud; listen to the *rhythm*, which is the important feature. As you read, ask yourself: Does your sentence have an orderly progression? Are the items balanced against each other? Do you like the way the paired words sound together?

NOTE: You can use other coordinating conjunctions besides *and* and *or.* See the fourth example below.

Examples

The textbook clearly showed the distinctions between prose and poetry, denotation and connotation, deduction and induction.

Great artists often seem to occur in pairs: Michelangelo and da Vinci, Gaugin and van Gogh, Monet and Cézanne.

Antony and Cleopatra, Romeo and Juliet, Tristan and Isolde, Lancelot and Guinevere were all famous lovers in literature.

Eager yet fearful, confident but somewhat suspicious, Jason eyed the barber who would give him his first haircut.

(This is a variation of the pattern.)

Professional examples

"A new book and PBS television series traces the numerous traditions—folk and gospel, blues and zydeco—that shaped American music."—*Smithsonian*, November 2001

"Smuin's recovery had much to do with changing his eating habits—after a lifetime of meat and potatoes and boxes of donuts and cold pizza at rehearsals—and his attitude toward life."— Cynthia Robins, *SF Chronicle Magazine*, December 10, 2001

"Tension is everywhere—kids at odds with parents, teachers, other kids and themselves; confused about life and love, popularity and principles, vitriol and virtue."—Susan Faust, *SF Chronicle*, October 28, 2001

"We will fashion 'crazy wisdom' from both secular and spiritual sources, both ancient and modern, and from both Eastern and Western cultures showing it to be the gritty core of many esoteric teachings and an essential part of the human story."—Wes "Scook" Nisker, *Crazy Wisdom*

"No man is really happy or safe without a hobby, and it makes precious little difference what the outside interest may be—botany, beetles, or butterflies; roses, tulips, or irises; fishing, mountaineering, or antiques—anything will do so long as he straddles a hobby and rides it hard."—Sir William Osler

NOTE: This sentence is a variation on a balanced series. Semicolons join the items of the series, which have internal punctuation.

Exercises

Complete each of the following sentences. Fill in the blanks with a series of balanced pairs.

1. Tea or coffee, _____ or

   _____ , _____

   or _____—these are popular drinks.

2. Some foods just seem to go together, like: _____

   and _____ .

3. Americans choose both a president and a vice president every four

   years; in the past we have chosen from _____

   and _____ , _____ and

   _____ and _____ .

4. Some Hollywood couples like _____

   and _____ or _____

   and _____ manage to have good marriages.

Using the words listed below, compose three sentences, each with a balanced series pattern:

1. oatmeal   Cheerios   coffee   tea   biscuits   honey

   _____

   _____

2. elephants   hippos   gorillas   monkeys

   _____

   _____

3. Veteran's Day   Labor Day   Mother's Day   Father's Day

   _____

   _____

As you read, watch for sentences that follow this pattern and add them below.

_____

_____

_____

_____

_____

_____

_____

_____

PATTERN 6:   AN INTRODUCTORY SERIES
                  OF APPOSITIVES
                  (with a dash and a summarizing subject)

Appositive, appositive, appositive— summary word S V.

(The key summarizing word before the subject may be one of these: *such, all, those, this, many, each, which, what, these, something, someone.* Sometimes this summary word will be the subject, but other times it will merely modify the subject.)

Explanation

This pattern begins with a "cluster" of appositives. An appositive is simply another word for something named elsewhere in the sentence—that is, it is another name for some noun. After the appositives, in sequence, you need a dash, a word that summarizes the appositives, and the subject-verb combination for the main clause. You may arrange the appositives in any of the patterns for series (see PATTERNS 4, 4a, and 5).

PATTERN 6 produces a highly stylized sentence, extremely effective for special places in your writing, places where you want to squeeze a lot of information into the same slot.

Examples

The depressed, the stressed, the lonely, the fearful—all have trouble coping with problems.

Gluttony, lust, envy—which is the worst sin?

Mickey Mouse, Magic Mountain, the Light Parade—these mean Disneyland to children.

Hawaiians, Filipinos, Japanese, Chinese—these ethnic groups make up much of Hawaii's diverse population.

Disko kloobs, verd processer, ti-shirti, konsulting, gala-konsert— these are some of the *Amerikanizatsia* of current Russian.

Bull riding, camel racing, bronc riding, and roping—these events mean "rodeo" to many people; they mean money to the cowboys.

(This example combines PATTERNS 1 and 6.)

The *Mona Lisa*, *Venus de Milo*, Egyptian mummies—what treasures the Louvre contains!

OR: —which of these is the best proof of the Italian imagination?

OR: —many are the wonders of the Renaissance in Italy.

An old photograph, a haunting fragrance, a sudden view of a half-forgotten scene—something unexpectedly triggers our nostalgia for the past.

NOTE: You can also put appositives at the end. Try reversing any of the sentences above, following the example below:

The tea tax, the lack of representation, the distance from the mother country, the growing sense of being a new and independent nation—what do you think caused the American Revolution?

What do you think caused the American Revolution—the tea tax, the lack of representation, the distance from the mother country, or the growing sense of being a new and independent nation?

Professional examples

"What it comes down to is this: the grocer, the butcher, the baker, the merchant, the landlord, the druggist, the liquor dealer, the policeman, the doctor, the city father and the politician—these are the people who make money out of prostitution, these are the real reapers of the wages of sin."—Polly Adler, *A House Is Not a Home*

"A car crash harnesses elements of eroticism, aggression, desire, speed, drama, kinaesthetic factors, the stylizing of motion, consumer goods, status—all these in one event."—J. G. Ballard, Interviews in *Penthouse*

Checkpoints

✓ Check the punctuation of this pattern:

1. you need commas between the appositives in the series;
2. you need a dash after the series.

✓ Check that you have a summary word at the beginning of the main clause.

✓ Check that, as in any series, all the appositives are parallel in structure and related in meaning.

Exercises

For each sentence supply introductory appositives that logically attach to the independent clause.

1. _____ , _____ ,

   _____ —each of these people served their

   country well.

2. To _____ , to _____ ,

   to _____ —such are the goals of the average

   American college graduate.

3. _____ or _____ ,

   _____ or _____ ,

   _____ or _____ —

   what are your preferences for spring break?

Complete each sentence by writing an appropriate summarizing word and independent clause.

1. Hardware, software, a modem—_____

   _____

   _____ .

2. Poetry and music, painting and sculpture, drama and dance —_____

   _____

   _____ .

As you read, watch for sentences that follow this pattern and add them below.

_____

_____

_____

_____

_____

_____

_____

_____

PATTERN 7:		AN INTERNAL SERIES OF APPOSITIVES OR MODIFIERS (enclosed by a pair of dashes or parentheses)			
<u>S</u>	$\overline{or}$ (	appositive, appositive, appositive modifier, modifier, modifier	$\overline{or}$)	<u>V</u>	

Explanation

You may have a series of appositives or modifiers (discussed in detail beginning on p. 61) anywhere in the sentence. Appositives will rename and modifiers will describe something named elsewhere in the sentence. Any kind of series (see PATTERNS 4, 4a, and 5) may come between the subject and the verb, between two subjects, and so on. Because this kind of series is a dramatic interruption within the sentence and may even have commas between the items, there *must* be a dash before and a dash after it.

You could also select parentheses to enclose the appositives or modifiers. Parentheses set off less important information. It is like an actor on stage whispering something to another character or to the audience in an aside (that is, conveying information not meant for everyone to hear).

Unlike an appositive, a modifier does not substitute for another word. Modifiers describe and give additional information about a single word or even a whole sentence. Although both modifiers and appositives are movable, a modifier must closely follow the word group it describes. If you place a modifier incorrectly, you may confuse your reader with a "dangling" construction (see PATTERN 12).

Examples

    S   V   DO

He learned the necessary qualities for political life—guile, ruthlessness, and garrulity—by carefully studying his father's life.

My favorite red wines—Zinfandel, Cabernet Sauvignon, Pinot Noir—blend well in making California rosé wines.

The basic writing skills (good vocabulary, knowledge of grammar, sense of style) can be learned by almost everyone.

(Try using dashes instead of parentheses in the sentence above. What subtle changes in meaning are suggested by the different punctuation choices?)

On our trip to Italy, the major sights—the Vatican in Rome, the Duomo in Florence, the tower in Pisa—didn't impress us as much as the food and the kindness of the people.

Many of the books kids enjoy reading (*Animal Farm, Catcher in the Rye, Harry Potter* novels) take them into another world.

The much-despised predators—mountain lions, timber wolves, and grizzly bears—have been shot, trapped, and poisoned so relentlessly for so long that they have nearly vanished from their old haunts.

Professional examples

"And then something happened which made her decide that Gregory Rowan was quite one of the most aggressive—and overbearing and unattractive—men she had ever encountered."—Antonia Fraser, *Cool Repentence*

"I was going on to relish more features of this unique scene: such as the advertisement posters on the walls—here a text from the bible, there a half-naked girl, here a woman wearing a hat consisting of a hen sitting on a nest full of eggs, and there a pair of girls' legs walking up the keys of a cash register—all scribbled over with unknown names and well-known obscenities . . ."—Gilbert Highet, "Subway Station"

Checkpoints

✓ You need a pair of dashes or parentheses to set off the modifier.

✓ If you take out the words between the dashes (or parentheses), do you still have a complete sentence? If so, you've used the punctuation correctly.

Exercises

Add an internal series of modifiers or appositives to complete each of the following sentences:

1. Which famous television personality—_____

_____ or _____ or

_____ —do you think will win this year's

Emmy Award?

2. The young gymnast—_____,

_____, and _____—

hoped to impress the judges.

3. Some television programs—_____ and

_____, and _____—

often help us relax.

Provide beginnings and endings to go with the following appositives or modifiers.

1. _____ —Spanish or French or Italian—

_____.

2. _____ —coordination, agility, speed—

_____.

3. _____ —lasagna and ravioli,

spaghetti and meatballs, spumoni and tortoni—_____

_____.

4. _____ —muscles, tan, good looks—

_____.

As you read, watch for sentences that follow this pattern and add them below.

_____

_____

_____

_____

_____

_____

_____

_____

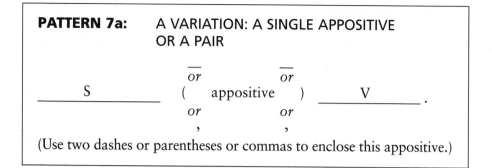

PATTERN 7a: A VARIATION: A SINGLE APPOSITIVE
OR A PAIR

$$
\underline{\qquad S \qquad}
\quad (\quad \text{appositive} \quad) \quad
\underline{\quad V \quad}.
$$

or ... *or*
or ... *or*
, ... ,

(Use two dashes or parentheses or commas to enclose this appositive.)

Explanation

This pattern resembles PATTERN 7 except it has only one or two apposi-tives instead of a full series. The appositive may or may not have modifiers. This variation has an interruption in thought immediately after the subject, but the appositive can have a variety of effects, depending on your punctuation:

a. a pair of dashes will make the appositive dramatic;

b. parentheses will make it almost whisper;

c. a pair of commas will make it nearly inconspicuous because they are so ordinary.

Examples

The sudden burst of light—a camera flash—startled me.

He recognized that smell—his mother's beef stew—and it imme-diately comforted him.

My latest desire, to go to Europe this summer, will have to wait until I get more money.

(In the sentence above, an infinitive modifies the subject and interrupts the subject-verb combination.)

Many people (especially ecologists) say that we need to do some-thing about global warming.

His ex-wife (once a famous Philadelphia model) now owns a well-known boutique in the Bahamas.

My grandfather's motto—take that extra step—guided him and now guides me.

The first man to walk on the moon, Neil Alden Armstrong, is a man the world will never forget.

Professional examples

"A century after his death, Giuseppi Verdi, the composer of *Aida* and *Il Trovatori*, still delights and enchants millions."—*Smithsonian*, November 2001

"Remington actually did use a camera to assist him with his illustrations, and he was an avid collector of Western props—Cavalry sabers, old rifles, Indian saddles, tomahawks, animal heads—which filled his large studio in New Rochelle, New York."—*National Geographic*, August 1988

Checkpoint

✓ Again, remember that you need TWO, not one, to make a pair—two dashes, a pair of parentheses, two commas.

Exercises

Fill in the blanks with a missing appositive or pair of appositives or other words to complete each sentence:

1. The familiar cheer of the football team—_____

   _____—began to appear on bumper

   stickers around the town.

2. _____ (my dog and cat)

   _____

   _____.

3. My favorite colors—_____ and

   _____—always attract me to new clothes.

4. Learning the basic skills—_____ and

   _____—will help me succeed in any sport.

5. _____ (plant shutdown) shocked the whole

   community.

Make up an original sentence using each of the following words as an interrupting appositive:

1. John F. Kennedy _____

_____

2. white wine _____

_____

3. personality _____

_____

As you read, watch for sentences that follow this pattern and add them below.

_____

_____

_____

_____

_____

_____

_____

_____

PATTERN 8: DEPENDENT CLAUSES IN A PAIR
OR IN A SERIES
(at beginning or end of sentence)

If . . . , if . . . , if . . . , _____ then ___ S ___ V ___ .

When . . . , when . . . , when . . . , S ___ V ___ .

___ S ___ V ___ that . . . , that . . . , that . . .   .

(omit the third clause and have just two, if you wish)

Explanation

The preceding patterns showed series with single words or phrases. PAT-
TERN 8 shows a different series with dependent clauses. All the clauses in
this series must be dependent. They must also be parallel in structure and
they must express conditions or situations or provisions dependent upon
the idea expressed in the main clause. The series may come at the beginning or at the end of the sentence. You will normally have two or three
clauses here; rarely will four or five sound graceful and smooth. Try not
to struggle for style; be natural, relaxed, never forced.

This pattern is unique. Save it for special places, special functions. It is
particularly helpful

a. at the end of a single paragraph to summarize the major points;

b. in structuring a thesis statement having three or more parts (or points);

c. in the introductory or concluding paragraph to bring together the
main points of a composition in a single sentence.

Examples

Because it may seem difficult at first, because it may sound awkward or forced, because it often creates lengthy sentences where the
thought "gets lost," this pattern seems forbidding to some writers,
but it isn't all that hard; try it.

If he had the money, if he had the time, if he had a companion, he
would take that trip around the world.

With no money and with no time, she had to refuse the vacation
package.

Whether you use a Mac or whether you use a PC, you can play great games on a computer.

I know that she was right, that her reasons were convincing and that I'd be better off if I did it, but I still didn't want to move to Canada.

Professional examples

"Though it was attached to a lead held by a man, and despite the fact that I had read in my book, *How and Why Wonder Book on Wild Animals,* that pumas do not usually harm people, I ran away as fast as I could."—*National Geographic,* June 1997

"If you attempt to save a chart before ever saving the supporting worksheet, Excel displays an alert box on the screen, asking you, in effect, if you are sure you want to proceed."—Douglas Hergert, *The ABC's of Excel on the Macintosh*

"Now, when I had mastered the language of this water, and had come to know every trifling feature that bordered the great river as familiarly as I knew the letters of the alphabet, I had made a valuable acquisition."—Mark Twain, *Life on the Mississippi*

"When you can measure what you are speaking about, and express it in numbers, you know something about it; but when you cannot measure it, when you cannot express it in numbers, your knowledge is of a meager and unsatisfactory kind."—William Thomson, Lord Kelvin

"I think of a city without cars, where dogs can dawdle, snuffing the wind; where everyone knows everyone else; where lions have wings; where cats and pigeons ignore one another; where people grow accustomed to living in a kind of sphere of absolute beauty, as if all of this were natural, whereas there is nothing at all natural about Venice."—Frederic Vitoux, "Life in Venice," *Travel and Life*

NOTE: The sentence above combines PATTERNS 8 and 9a.

Sentence for analysis

Do you think this sentence is effective stylistically? Does the tone complement the content?

"I wish I could say that I discovered Arden in some appropriately romantic fashion—that my Land Rover was stopped by hooded archers in a bosky byway; that I was kidnapped by free-love agitators on a dark and stormy night; or that I tracked a fugitive Soviet coup meister to a secret Stalinist camp in the Delaware woods."—Henry Wiencek, *Smithsonian,* May 1992

_____

_____

Checkpoints

✓ You don't always need three dependent clauses here. Two will also work in this pattern.

✓ Whether you have only two or a full series of three or more, whether you have the clauses at the beginning or the end of the sentence, arrange them in some order of increasing impact.

Exercises

Fill in the blanks to construct logical dependent or independent clauses:

1. If your teacher says to read it twice, if _____,

   or if _____, you'd better follow your teacher's

   wishes rather than your friend's.

2. When _____,

   when the astronaut heard the explosion, when the air controller

   _____ , then the flight crew

   _____ .

3. The new puppy _____

   because _____

   and because _____ .

4. Whether you think _____

   or whether you think _____ , you

   _____ .

5. The basketball coach shouted that the referee _____,

_____, that the other team's coach

_____, and that

_____.

As you read, watch for sentences that follow this pattern and add them below.

_____

_____

_____

_____

_____

_____

_____

_____

REPETITIONS

PATTERNS 9 and 9a address repetition. Before we discuss the patterns, let's look at the importance of repetition in our writing.

WHAT ARE REPETITIONS?

A repetition is a restatement of a term; you may repeat the term once or several times within a sentence or a paragraph.

WHY USE REPETITIONS?

Repetitions help to echo key words, to emphasize important ideas or main points, to unify sentences, or to develop coherence among sentences. Skillful repetitions of important words or phrases create "echoes" in the reader's mind: they emphasize and point out key ideas. You can use these "echo words" in different sentences—even in different paragraphs—to help "hook" your ideas together. Avoid meaningless repetition—it might suggest mental laziness or an inadequate vocabulary.

HOW DO YOU CREATE REPETITIONS?

You can allow an important word to recur in a sentence or in a paragraph or even in different paragraphs. These echo words may come any place in the sentence: with the subjects or the verbs, with the objects or the complements, with prepositions or other parts of speech. You need not always repeat the word exactly; think of other forms the word may take, such as *freak, freakiness, freakishness* (nouns), *freaking* (participle), *freaky* and *freakish* (adjectives), and *freakishly* and *freakily* (adverbs).

WHERE IS REPETITION APPROPRIATE?

Repetition is appropriate:

a. in different positions in the same sentence (PATTERN 9);

b. in the same position (or "slot") of the sentence: for example, the same preposition is repeated in a series or the same word is used as object of different prepositions (PATTERN 9a).

   NOTE: Once you have mastered repetitions in the same sentence, you will be ready to repeat some key words or phrases throughout your paragraphs, even from one paragraph to the next. In your reading, look for the many ways that writers effectively repeat some of their key words, placing them in strategic positions in the sentence and throughout the same paragraph. In one paragraph Rachel Carson used *sea* ten times; throughout one dramatic speech Winston Churchill repeated the sentence "We shall fight" eight times, using it to emphasize various points. Martin Luther King, Jr., used this technique most effectively in his "I Have a Dream" speech.

HOW DOES PUNCTUATION AFFECT YOUR MESSAGE?

Commas, dashes, periods, colons, and semicolons signal varying degrees of pause. A comma marks a brief pause; a dash signals a longer one. Pauses created by the colon, the semicolon, and the period have a ring of finality. The colon suggests that important words will follow. The semicolon (like the period) signals a full stop before another idea begins.

You have probably noticed that, in all explanations (including the graphic displays that introduce each pattern), spacing before and after punctuation marks has been deliberately exaggerated so that you will pay attention to the important punctuation. When you imitate each pattern, however, you will want to use traditional spacing before and after punctuation as in all example sentences. Use two hyphens to distinguish a **dash** (—) from a **hyphen** (-).

When choosing between a comma and a dash, use this guideline to determine the type of pause you need: a **comma** signals a very brief pause (it is as though you have hiccupped right in the middle of your thought); a **dash** makes you take a longer breath. A **period, colon, question mark,** or **exclamation point** requires you to pause, take a deep breath, then allows you to continue. (See also "Why Punctuate?" on page 145.)

Consider these differences; decide what kind of pause you need; then punctuate, remembering that the various marks are not interchangeable. Each suggests a different kind of pause. In following three sentences, how does the punctuation change the impact and tone of the message?

> Homer, if there was a single "Homer," probably never "wrote" a word of *The Iliad*.

> Homer (if there was a single "Homer") probably never "wrote" a word of *The Iliad*.

> Homer—if there was a single "Homer"—probably never "wrote" a word of *The Iliad*.

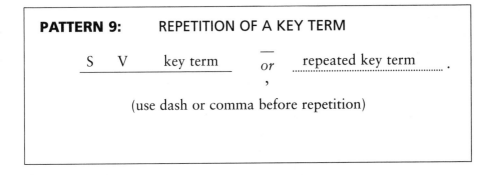

Explanation

In this pattern you repeat a key word in a modifying phrase attached to the main clause. You may repeat the word exactly as it is, or you may use another form: *brute* may become *brutal*; *breath* may become *breath-taking*; *battle* may become *battling*.

The key term is a word important enough to be repeated. It can come anywhere in the sentence, but usually comes at the end. Or, if you have a key word in the subject slot, the repetition may be, for example, a part of an interrupting modifier.

You may vary this pattern slightly by using a dash instead of a comma. The dash suggests a longer pause, a greater break in thought than the comma does.

NOTE 1: Be sure that the word is worth repeating. Notice how in-effective the following sentence is because of the repetition of the uninteresting, overworked word:

> He was a good father, providing a good home for his good children.

NOTE 2: Be sure that the attached phrase with the repeated key term is NOT a complete sentence; if it is, you will create a comma splice, as here:

> He was a cruel brute of a man, he was brutal to his family and even more brutal to his friends.

Here's one way of correcting the comma splice:

> He was a cruel brute of a man, brutal to his family and even more brutal to his friends.

Examples

We live in an uncertain world—the inner world, the world of the mind.

A. E. Housman used this PATTERN 9 at the end of a famous lecture: "The tree of knowledge will remain forever, as it was in the beginning, a tree to be desired to make one wise."

We all have problems but we can find a solution, a solution that works, a solution that is equitable.

She suddenly felt filled with joy—a joy she could not explain but that she gladly embraced.

The warning in the tarot cards—an ominous warning about the dangers of air flight—could not deter Marsha from volunteering for the first Mars shot.

Professional examples

"Privacy, of course, has the advantage of, well, privacy."—Susin Shapiro, *Lear's,* April 1993

"A spectre is haunting Europe—the spectre of Communism."— Karl Marx, "The Communist Manifesto"

"The man for whom law exists—the man of forms, the conservative—is a tame man."—Henry David Thoreau, *Journal,* May 30, 1861

"All progress is precarious and the solution to one problem brings us face to face with another problem."—Martin Luther King, Jr., *Strength to Love*

Checkpoints

✓✓ Double check! The repetition must be a phrase, not a clause. In this pattern, the words following the dash or comma MUST NOT have a subject or a verb with the repeated word; the result would be a comma splice (comma fault).

WRONG: He was part of the older generation, his generation was born before the Depression. (This compound must have a semicolon.)

CORRECT: He was part of the older generation, a generation born before the Depression.

Another error might occur when you use a period or semicolon where the comma should be. That creates a fragment out of the modifier containing the repeated key term.

WRONG: He praises the beauty of his love. A love that is unfortunately hopeless because it is not mutual.

NOTE: This example contains the "pattern" of a very common fragment error:

<u>   S   V   </u> . <u> S + [dep. clause] but NO verb. </u>

CORRECT: He praises the beauty of his love, a love unfortunately hopeless because it is not mutual.

Exercises

Complete each of the following sentences by repeating the underlined word.

1. The floats in the parade were <u>stunning</u>, stunning in _____

_____ , stunning also in

_____ .

2. <u>Courteous</u>—courteous to _____

_____ , courteous to _____

_____—the prom committee managed to

smooth all the tense situations.

3. The faithful worshipers believed the religious leader to be a <u>compassionate</u> man, compassionate to _____ .

Develop original sentences, repeating in each one a word that ends in *-ing*, similar to the sentences above.

1. _____

_____ .

2. _____

_____ .

As you read, watch for sentences that follow this pattern and add them below.

_____

_____

_____

_____

_____

_____

_____

_____

> **PATTERN 9a:** A VARIATION:
> SAME WORD REPEATED IN
> PARALLEL STRUCTURE
>
> S V repeated key word in same position of the sentence.

Explanation

You can use repetitions in other ways, of course.

1. You may repeat an effective adjective or adverb in phrases or clauses with parallel construction:

> She has an incredibly satisfying life, satisfying because of her career and satisfying because of her family.

2. You may repeat the same preposition in a series:

> He has known her for many years, before she went to college, before she was a star, before she won the Oscar.

3. You may repeat the same noun as the object of different prepositions:

> This government is of the *people*, by the *people*, and for the *people*.

4. You may repeat the same modifying word in phrases that begin with different prepositions:

> Sidney devoted his life to those *selfish* people, for their *selfish* cause, but clearly with his own *selfish* motives dominating his every action.

5. You may repeat the same intensifiers:

> The baseball game was very exciting, very enjoyable, but very long.

6. You may repeat the same verb or alternative forms of the same word:

> In order to survive in war, a person needs training, a person needs courage, and, most of all, a person needs luck.

Examples

> Rodin's *The Thinker* presents the perfect figure in the perfect pose.
>
> If you have unrealistic dreams, you may need to find other goals, other desires.

Venice presents great gifts to the visitor—great history, great art, great crafts.

His greatest discoveries, his greatest successes, his greatest influence upon the world's daily life came to Edison only after repeated failure.

Professional examples

"In a few minutes the second twin gathered all his legs and all his ingenuity and arose, to stand for the first time sniffing the mysteries of a park for captive deer."—E. B. White, "Twins"

"Tolerance, good temper and sympathy are no longer enough in a world which is rent by religious and racial persecution, in a world where ignorance rules. . . . Tolerance, good temper and sympathy —they are what matter really—and if the human race is not to collapse they must come to the front before long."—E. M. Forster, "What I Believe"

"We are fond of saying that something is not just something but 'a way of life'; this too is a way of life—our way, the way."—Randall Jarrell, "A Sad Heart at the Supermarket"

"It is (the book) about ulcers as well as accidents, about shouting matches as well as fistfights, about nervous breakdowns as well as kicking the dog around."—Studs Terkel, *Working*

Exercises

Expand each of the following basic sentences by repeating one of the modifying words in a phrase.

1. Your grandmother was right: there is nothing new under the sun,

   nothing _____ , only

   _____ .

2a. But these numbers tell only part of the story, only _____

   _____ , only

   _____ , only

   _____ .

b. (Rewrite the same sentence but this time repeat the word *part.*) But these numbers tell only part of the story, part _____ _____, part _____ .

3a. The Western world possesses awesome amounts of virtually untapped resources, awesome _____, awesome _____ .

b. (Rewrite the same sentence but repeat the word *untapped.*) The Western world possesses awesome amounts of virtually untapped resources, untapped _____, untapped _____ .

c. (Rewrite the same sentence but this time repeat the word *resources.*) The Western world possesses awesome amounts of virtually untapped resources, resources _____, resources _____, resources _____, resources _____ .

As you read, watch for sentences that follow this pattern and add them below.

_____

_____

_____

_____

_____

_____

_____

_____

PATTERN 10:	EMPHATIC APPOSITIVE AT END, AFTER A COLON

S   V   word :   the appositive (the second naming) .

(with or without modifiers)

Explanation

Often you want to repeat an idea, not just a word. Withholding the repetition until the end of the sentence builds to a climax and provides a forceful, emphatic appositive that concludes the sentence and practically shouts for your reader's attention. In the above pattern, the colon—because it is formal and usually comes before a rather long appositive—emphasizes this climax. Remember that the colon marks a full stop and therefore must come only after a complete statement; it tells the reader that important words or an explanation will follow.

Also, if you want to give a repeated word greater stress, you can make it into an appositive and signal its importance by a preceding colon. Note that here only a single word follows, unlike PATTERN 3, which has an entire sentence after the colon. Now compare three similar PATTERNS—3, 10, and 10a—and note the differences in both the structures and the appropriate times when you would use them to achieve unique effects.

Examples

Her room contained a collection of trash: old clothes, soda cans, McDonald's wrappers.

When I go to the movies, I need two things to really enjoy it: popcorn and a soda.

Airport thieves have a common target: unwary travelers.

Professional examples

"In perpetrating a revolution, there are two requirements: someone or something to revolt against and someone to actually show up and do the revolting."—Woody Allen, "A Brief, Yet Helpful Guide to Civil Disobedience"

"Only cats would likely approve of one old-fashioned remedy for cuts: a lotion of catnip, butter, and sugar."—Lynn Quitman Troyka, *Handbook for Writers*

"The hair coat in the cat consists of three different types of hair: primary or guard hairs within the outer coat; awn hairs (intermediate-sized hairs forming part of the primary coat); and secondary hairs (downy hairs found in the undercoat)."—John Saidla, Cornell Feline Health Center

NOTE: Once again, the series has internal punctuation and needs semicolons.

Sentence for analysis

Analyze the following sentence, looking for repetitions, sentence patterns, punctuation, and content. In the space provided, jot down your reaction to the sentence—its length, clarity, and rhetorical effectiveness.

"They avoided talk about the deceased's final year, about how he had been transfigured by drugs in a losing battle against an inoperable brain tumor, about how he was reduced from a trim, combative five-mile-a-day runner to a frail man in a wheelchair, his head swollen with chemicals, his eyes hollow with defeat and sadness."—*American Way,* January 1992

_____

_____

_____

Checkpoints

✓ Check the words *before* the colon; be sure they make a full statement (sentence).

✓ After the colon, be sure to write only a word or a phrase—not a full statement. See PATTERN 3.

Exercises

Supply the missing parts for the following sentences. Each sentence should include an emphatic appositive.

1. _____

an "A," the grade I really had worked for.

2. (Make up a sentence with a person's name as the emphatic appositive.)

_____ :

_____ .

(name)

3. The class elected _____

as treasurer: Jim Rutledge.

4. _____ award:

_____ , the most coveted

of all _____ distinctions.

5a. (Make up a sentence with an emphatic single-word appositive. After the appositive use a prepositional phrase to modify it.)

_____ :

_____ .

(appositive plus prepositional phrase)

b. (Rewrite the sentence in *a* and make the emphatic appositive into an infinitive phrase. Remember that an infinitive consists of *to* and the base form of a verb, as in *to squirm*.)

_____ :

to _____ .

(infinitive phrase)

c. (Now, repeating the same idea as in *a* and *b* above, modify the emphatic appositive with a word group beginning with *-ing* or an *-en* or *-ed* word—that is, a *present* or *past* tense participle.)

_____ :

_____ .

(*-ing*, *-en*, or *-ed* word)

As you read, watch for sentences that follow this pattern and add them below.

_____

_____

_____

_____

_____

_____

_____

_____

PATTERN 10a: A VARIATION: APPOSITIVE
(single or pair or series)
AFTER A DASH

<u>S   V   word</u> —   the appositive   .

(echoed idea or second naming)

Explanation

For variation, you may use a dash instead of a colon before a short, emphatic appositive at the end of a sentence. Notice that in both PATTERNS 10 and 10a, the second naming is usually climactic or emphatic. The difference is only in punctuation: a dash almost always precedes a short, climactic appositive, whereas a colon generally precedes a longer appositive. (Contrast PATTERN 9 with PATTERN 10a.)

Study the differences in sound and emphasis that the punctuation and the length of the appositive make in the following sentences:

Adjusting to a new job requires one quality, humor.

(common usage but not emphatic)

Adjusting to a new situation requires one quality: humor.

(significant pause, but not so dramatic)

Adjusting to a new job requires one quality above all others—a sense of humor.

(dramatic signaling)

Adjusting to a new job requires one quality: the ability to laugh at oneself.

(more dramatic, more stylistically complete)

Examples

Many traditional philosophies echo the ideas of one man—Plato.

Pandas eat only one food—bamboo shoots.

Those big burgers taste great but they have lots of calories—over 1,000.

E-mail is wonderful and so easy to send but also represents a major problem—answering it.

The grasping of seaweeds reveals the most resourceful part of the sea horse—its prehensile tail.

Professional examples

"From the very beginning, Boswell had an imaginative conception of Johnson, different from that of anyone else who knew him, as a hero who is also a great comic character—the Falstaff of the intellect."—Adam Gopnik, *New Yorker*, November 27, 2000

"It's not surprising then, that many sociologists believe we are a nation of substance abusers—drinkers, smokers, overeaters, and pill poppers."—Alfred Rosa and Paul Eschholz

"The reader is someone with an attention span of about 10 seconds—a person assailed by other forces competing for attention."—William Zinsser, "Simplicity"

"Charles Darwin and Abraham Lincoln were both born on the same day—February 12, 1809. They were also linked in another curious way—for both men must simultaneously play, and for similar reasons, the role of man and legend."—Stephen Jay Gould

Checkpoints

✓ Keep in mind that the second naming must be a true appositive; don't just "stick in" a dash or a colon before you get to the end of the sentence. If you do, you may simply create an error in punctuation, not a true appositive. Here is an example, lifted from a student's paper:

POOR: One class of teenagers can be labeled—students.

CORRECT: One label would fit almost any teenager—student.

✓ Remember that a dash cannot separate two complete thoughts. Avoid a "dash splice."

WRONG: Mary Shelley spent a full year at Marlow writing *Frankenstein*—her monster has survived better than some of her husband's poems.

CORRECT: Mary Shelley spent a full year at Marlow writing *Frankenstein*—creating a monster that has survived better than some of her husband's poems.

Exercises

Rewrite each of the following sentences so that it ends with a dramatic appositive after a dash. You may need to add, delete, or rearrange words.

1. *War and Peace*, one of the world's masterpieces, covers Napoleon Bonaparte's crucial campaign, an invasion of Russia by the largest army ever assembled from twenty nations.

   _____

   _____

   _____

2. The thesis of *War and Peace*, as stated by Tolstoy, is that the course of the greatest historical events is determined ultimately not by military leaders, but by conventional people.

   _____

   _____

   _____

Compose or rewrite sentences as directed below:

1. (Supply the missing dramatic appositive.) The destiny of nations is

   controlled by the common people—_____

   _____.

2a. (Make up a sentence ending with a dramatic single-word appositive

   after a dash.) _____—

   _____.
   (single word)

 b. (Rewrite the sentence, ending it with a dramatic prepositional

   phrase) _____

   _____—_____.
   (prepositional phrase)

 c. (Again rewrite the sentence, ending it with a dramatic infinitive

   phrase.) _____—

   _____.
   (infinitive phrase)

d. (Now repeat the same idea, using an *-ing* or an *-en* word or phrase at the beginning of the dramatic appositive.) _____

_____ —

_____ .

(-ing or -en word here)

As you read, watch for sentences that follow this pattern and add them below.

_____

_____

_____

_____

_____

_____

_____

_____

MODIFIERS

To clarify a sentence that is too brief or general, you can add modifiers. A key word may need more explanation—one or more modifiers—to make its meaning clear:

> The lovely model—tall, blonde, graceful—captured the audience.

Modifiers can be single words, phrases, even clauses, and may be anywhere in the sentence. A good way to use them is to take two short sentences and make one of them a dependent clause modifier:

> CHANGE: My coach is always fair. He gives us all a chance to play.

> TO: My coach, always fair, gives us all a chance to play.

Modifiers work well when you want to appeal to a reader's senses or use some figurative language. Be careful. Remember that the modifier clings to the nearest target. If your modifier clings to the wrong target, you wind up with a silly sentence. For example:

> Carrying a heavy pile of books, his foot caught on the steps.

> (It sounds as if his foot was carrying a heavy pile of books.)

Appositives, which rename the subject, are another form of modifier:

> My sister, an English professor, teaches at Stanford.

A special use for the appositive is as a modifier for a whole sentence where it renames an idea in the sentence:

> To speak freely, to bear arms, to vote—these are freedoms we often take for granted.

PATTERN 11: INTERRUPTING MODIFIER
BETWEEN S AND V

S , modifier , V .

S — modifier — V .

S (modifier that whispers) V .

Explanation

When a modifier comes between the subject and the verb, you may separate it from the main elements of the sentence with a pair of commas or a pair of dashes. For variety, if the modifier is merely an aside within the sentence (a kind of whisper), put parentheses around it. This modifier can be a single word, a pair of words, or even a phrase that provides additional information, as in the examples below.

In this pattern, the punctuation sets off the modifier dramatically. You would use this pattern when you believe dramatic signaling is appropriate, as you do in PATTERNS 10 and 10a. The difference in PATTERN 11 is that the word stressed is a modifier rather than an appositive. Also, note that, depending on the type of emphasis you want to give the modifier, you can choose a pair of commas, a pair of dashes, or parentheses.

Examples

A small drop of ink, falling (as Byron said) like dew upon a thought, can make millions think.

Donuts and Danish pastries, popular breakfast foods, contain little nutrition.

Typewriters, once common in schools and offices, are rarely seen or used now.

Wolves—once feared and killed—are being reintroduced into the environment.

Relaxation and informality are important parts of our fantasies about life in a tropical paradise, and once you get accustomed to having twenty people waiting on you hand and foot (it doesn't take very long), you no longer feel like a guest.

American fast food has certainly taken hold, especially among young people of Singapore, and steak houses (not to mention McDonald's and Kentucky Fried Chicken) are familiar sights along Orchard Road.

Professional examples

"Sometimes children from other classes, those presumably not so intellectually gifted, would tease and taunt us."—Michael T. Kaufman, "Of My Friend Hector and My Achilles Heel"

"I guess I couldn't read anything at all then—not even my own name—and they tell me I didn't talk as good as other kids."—David Raymond, "On Being 17, Bright, and Unable to Read"

"Nearly every inauguration, from that of a Pope or a President down to that of a restaurant manager or a platoon sergeant, is followed by a honeymoon period. . . ."—Theodore Caplow, *How to Run Any Organization*

"Women, who are still free from being expected to know anything about their vehicles, are nevertheless just as passionate in their relationship with them as men are, and at times just as wonderfully irrational."—Ken "Babyface" Rogers, Producer for "Car Talk" on NPR

Sentence for analysis

In the following sentence, why did the writer use parentheses? What impact do they have on you? How important is the material within the parentheses? Note the capitalization *after* the colon.

"It is still possible to live like a maharaja (although it's not quite as comfortable as one might wish): Simply book passage on the Maharaja of Jodhpur's private railcar, the last royal train remaining in India."—*Condé Nast Traveler*, September 1992

_____

_____

_____

_____

Checkpoint

✓ Remember that the punctuation marks for this pattern must go in pairs, with one mark before the modifier and one after it.

Exercises

Add additional information and descriptions of the subjects in the following sentences by providing interrupting modifiers or other missing parts. (Review the exercises for PATTERNS 7 and 7a, to determine the difference between an interrupting appositive and an interrupting modifier before you begin this exercise.)

1. My Valentine's Day gift, _____,

_____.

2. _____ —like the fire of an opal—

_____.

3. _____, enjoyable yet not unexpected,

_____.

4. The poses of the model (_____

_____) were almost

_____.

5. (Use this sentence for the exercises below.) The political candidate learned the results of the Michigan primary.

 a. (Provide **one** or **two** words ending in *-en* as the interrupting modifier.) The political candidate, _____,

 learned the results of the Michigan primary.

 b. (Provide **two** words ending in *-ing* as the interrupting modifier.) The political candidate—_____—learned

 the results of the Michigan primary.

c. (Provide a modifier in **parentheses** that whispers.) The political candidate (_____) learned the results of the Michigan primary.

As you read, watch for sentences that follow this pattern and add them below.

_____

_____

_____

_____

_____

_____

_____

_____

PATTERN 11a: A FULL SENTENCE
(statement or question or exclamation)
AS INTERRUPTING MODIFIER

—a full sentence—

S   *or*   V   .

(a full sentence)

Explanation

The modifier that interrupts the main thought may be a full sentence—a statement, a question, or an exclamation. If it is, do not put a period before the second dash unless the statement is a quotation. If the sentence is a question or an exclamation, you will need punctuation. A question mark or an exclamation point may seem strange in the middle of a sentence, but this pattern requires such punctuation.

The interrupting modifier does not always come between the subject and the verb. (See the last three examples below.) And notice the different signals that the punctuation gives the reader. Parentheses, as in other patterns, really say that the material enclosed is simply an aside, not very important. Dashes here, however, indicate that the interrupter is important to a complete understanding of some word in the sentence.

Examples

Juliet's famous question—early in the balcony scene she asks, "Wherefore art thou Romeo?"—is often misunderstood; she meant not "where," but "why."

One of Thoreau's most famous analogies—"If a man does not keep pace with his companions, perhaps it is because he hears a different drummer. Let him step to the music he hears, however measured or far away."—echoes Shakespeare's advice that we should be true to ourselves.

NOTE: Here the statement before the dash is a quotation, and the period is correct.

He leaped at the chance (too impetuously, I thought) to go white-water rafting.

NOTE: Here the interrupting modifier comes *after* the verb.

Although the young models looked wonderful in their new $500 parkas—they were pretending to know how to ski—not one of them dared venture down the giant slalom.

Narcissus ignored Echo so completely (how could he? she was such a lovely nymph!) that she just faded away.

Professional examples

"If you are having trouble with your conclusion—and this is not an uncommon occurrence—it may be because of problems with your essay itself."—Alfred Rosa and Paul Eschholz, *Models for Writers*

"The excreta gets into his [the koala bear's] gut—you know, he's got about 20 foot of gut in there, it's all over the place—and starts his stomach working so he can break down the stuff that's poisonous."—Oliver Payne, *National Geographic*, April 1995

"All that a pacifist can undertake—but it is a very great deal—is to refuse to kill, injure, or otherwise cause suffering to another human creature."—Vera Brittain, "What Can We Do in Wartime?"

"They were being careful, but American ingenuity—our nation is one of the world leaders in land mine technology—has made even looking for land mines a dangerous proposition."—Jon Carroll, *SF Chronicle*, December 25, 2001

Sentence to analyze

In the following sentence note how the writer uses parentheses to enclose both whole sentences and single modifiers. Observe also that the author makes a general comment, then follows with quotations from John Jerome's book as specific illustrations enclosed in parentheses. Do you find the punctuation distracting, helpful, or effective?

"In lively, thoughtful entries Jerome tells stories about his writing career (like the time the editor of *Esquire* summoned him in to save the October issue); ponders language ("Punctuation is nails, screws, nuts and bolts, the means by which you secure things in place."); tells how to start a book proposal ("Imagine that the book-to-be gets onto the *Times* best seller list, then write the two-line summary that would run with its listing."); exults over good reviews ("more dancing around the kitchen"); and talks about his work in progress."—"The Writing Trade," *BOMC News*, February 1992

_____

_____

_____

Checkpoint

✓ Use this pattern with restraint. Otherwise, your reader may think you have a "grasshopper mind" and can't finish one thought without interference from another.

Exercises

Supply the missing parts for the following sentences, keeping in mind that for PATTERN 11a the modifier must be a sentence:

1. The scary movie (I know _____!)

   _____ .

2. My favorite question—"What's in it for me?"—_____

   _____ .

3. My new Guess jeans—_____

   _____—seemed out of place

   at the party.

4. _____ (it dates back to the

   1980s, at least) _____ .

5. Generally thought to be of Dutch origin, the tulip—_____

   _____—originally came

   from central Asia.

As you read, watch for sentences that follow this pattern and add them below.

_____

_____

_____

_____

_____

_____

_____

_____

PATTERN 12:   INTRODUCTORY OR CONCLUDING
                  PARTICIPLES

Participial phrase   ,   _____S____V_____   .

____S_____V_____   ,   Participial phrase   .

Explanation

As we have seen, modifiers come in a variety of forms—single words, groups of words (phrases), even clauses. One unique kind is the participial modifier, a verb form that, used as a single word or as part of a phrase, functions as a modifier. Participles have three forms:

> *present*   (ending in *-ing*)
>
> *past*   (normally ending in *-d* or *-ed*)
>
> *irregular*   (so *irregular* that you will have to memorize these!)

Example

> Persevering, determined to succeed, driven by wanderlust, blest with discipline, the pioneers forged a civilization out of a wilderness.
>
> | | |
> |---:|---|
> | *Persevering* | (present regular) |
> | *determined* | (past regular) |
> | *driven* | (past irregular) |
> | *blest* | (past irregular) |

The dictionary is a good resource if you are unsure of irregular participial forms. Remember that all participles function as adjectives, modifying nouns. Also, you can place participial modifiers at the beginning or the end of a sentence as long as it is absolutely clear what they modify.

In the following sentences, note how shifting the movable participial phrase to various positions creates subtle changes in meaning or emphasis. Does the second example work as well as the first or third one? If you set off the participial phrase in example two with a pair of commas, what would the sentence be saying? Would its meaning change as a result of the commas? Remember, when you set off modifiers with a pair of commas or other punctuation, you tell your reader this material is not really needed to communicate the main message.

Guarding us with their powerful guns, the heavily armed soldiers at the Rio conference looked ominous.

The heavily armed soldiers guarding us with their powerful guns at the Rio conference looked ominous.

NOTE: Here the phrase is *restrictive* or *essential,* suggesting that specific soldiers were guarding us. See in the following example how the phrase is commentary and thus *nonrestrictive.*

The heavily armed soldiers at the Rio conference, guarding us with their powerful guns, looked ominous.

Once you are familiar with what a participle is, PATTERN 12 will be simple. Although participial modifiers may come at the beginning and at the end of the sentence, they may also come as interrupters at any point.

CAUTION: Do not dangle participles! Be sure to place them next to the word they modify. You will have no trouble with them if you remember not to "shift subjects" at the comma: The subject of your sentence must be the idea or person you describe in the modifying phrase, not some other person or word. Inadvertent danglers usually result in unintentional humor or illogical statements, like the following:

Walking onto the stage, the spotlight followed the singer.

Overgrown with moss, the gardener cleaned his seed flats for spring planting. (Overgrown with moss is the participial phrase here.)

The three boys tried to steal my bike while going on an errand.

The man in the advertisement is shown standing in the middle of a stream holding an ax surrounded by trees.

See examples below for modifiers that don't dangle.

Examples

The man failed the driver's test given that he did not study at all.

NOTE: *Given* is the participle here.

Expecting a spectacular display, the crowd eagerly awaited the fireworks.

Inspired by the reach of the woods and the magnificent view, he was able to finish his novel.

Printed in Old English and bound in real leather, the new edition of *Beowulf* was too expensive for the family to buy.

NOTE: *Printed* and *bound* are the participles here.

Professional examples

"Standing at the very center of those paradoxes, the old Taoists shrugged and let out a sigh of relief, accepting that they could not resolve them."—Wes "Scoop" Risker, *Crazy Wisdom*

"Running in and out of the sun, you met what seemed total obscurity inside."—Eudora Welty, "The Corner Stone"

"Faced with such obstacles, readers are at first tenacious."—William Zinsser, "Simplicity"

"Sprawled on the sofa, I finally faced up to the grim task, took the list out of my notebook, and scanned it."—Russell Baker, "Becoming a Writer"

Sentence for analysis

In the following sentences, locate the participial modifiers. Do they work well?

Appearing on television talk shows, crisscrossing the country on the campus lecture circuit, invited to be on important programs, fad theorists and former criminals become the darlings of our society before we forget and discard them for others.

_____

_____

_____

Exercises

Try these exercises:

1. (Rewrite the following sentence, beginning it with an *-ed* word.) If you

   water your African violets carefully, they will burst into bloom.

   _____

   _____

2. (Rewrite the following sentence, beginning it with an *-ed* or *-en* word.) The underdog team, the Braves, beat the Giants, but the Giants won the World Series. _____

_____

3. (Supply the missing words in this sentence. Begin with an *-ing* word.)

_____ the student

skipped his next class.

4. (Begin the following sentence with an *-ed* word. Follow the *-ed* word with one *-ly* modifier.) _____

_____ , the child finally dozed off to sleep.

5. (Supply the missing words in the sentence. Begin with an *-ing* word. Follow the *-ing* word with an *-ly* word.) _____

_____ , the cheetah leaped from the lower branch

to the top of the tree.

6. (Rewrite the following sentence with a participial phrase at the *end*.) The people on the bus obeyed the driver's instructions. _____

_____

_____

7. (Supply the missing words in this sentence. Begin the missing word group with an *-ing* word.) Spring weather always brightens my spirits _____

_____.

As you read, watch for sentences that follow this pattern and add them below.

```
PATTERN 13:    A SINGLE MODIFIER OUT
               OF PLACE FOR EMPHASIS

               Modifier            ,      S     V      .
               ........................................
               (modifier may be in other positions)
```

Explanation

To place additional emphasis on any modifier, put it somewhere other than its normal place in the sentence. Sometimes, in this new position, the modifier seems so normal that it sounds clear without a comma; at other times, you *must* have a comma to keep the reader from misinterpreting your sentence. For example:

As a whole, people tend to be happy.

(Otherwise, "As a whole people . . .")

To begin with, some ideas are difficult.

(Otherwise, "To begin with some ideas . . .")

Sometimes a single word such as *before, inside,* or *below* may look like a preposition instead of an adverb if you forget the comma in a sentence like this one:

Inside, the child was noisy.

Now look what internal rumblings you create when you have no comma:

Inside the child was noisy.

If a modifier is clearly an adverb, however, you may not need the comma:

Later the child was quiet.

One pitfall in writing sentences has always been the split infinitive—inserting a modifier between the "to" and the "verb" (such as "to boldly leap"), and this pattern can help you avoid this faulty construction. In recent years, however, the split infinitive is considered acceptable in casual writing but is still frowned upon in formal writing. In the following sentence *occasionally* would be better at the beginning than where it is, separating the two parts of the infinitive and *further* should follow *illustrate.*

Francesca liked *to occasionally wade* in the neighbor's pool.

The professor tried *to further illustrate* the point of the essay.

Examples

Below, the traffic looked like a necklace of ants.

Desperate, the young mother called for help.

Frantic, the young hiker rushed over with the rescue rope.

The general demanded absolute obedience, instant and unquestioning.

All day the walkers sweated in the sun, pleased that they were walking for a good cause—preventing breast cancer.

Professional examples

"Extradited, he got similar adulation, as he passed through Concord, New Hampshire."—*Smithsonian*, February 1999

"Delirious, she cried out for her children and apologized for an accident she neither caused nor could have avoided."—Ruth Russell, "The Wounds That Can't Be Stitched Up"

"Unhappy the land that is in need of heroes."—Bertolt Brecht, "The Life of Galileo"

"Now French Protestants—heretics—squatted in Philip's Florida." —Richard and Joyce Welkomir, *Smithsonian*, October 2001

Sentences for analysis

1. Occasionally authors can show an emotional reaction to their material. In the following sentence look for ways that David Segal conveys his emotional stance (*tone*). In describing the manner of Lynne Cheney, Segal interrupts the second clause with the modifier *well*. How does this carefully placed *well* suggest Segal's attitude toward Cheney's policies?

   "Cheney denies that she meddles; in my interview with her, she describes herself as, well, helpful."—David Segal, *Lingua Franca*

---

2. How is *well* used, stylistically, in the dependent clause of this sentence? "And there is a certain spaciousness, a 'swagger' in these works, that seems, well, American."—J. E. Vacha, *American Heritage*, September 1992

_____

_____

_____

Exercises

Revise each of the following sentences so that a modifier you want to emphasize comes at the beginning.

1. Rodeos began as rough-and-ready contests among rival cowboys to settle long-festering differences. _____

_____

_____

2. Rodeos are a multimillion-dollar business now in all parts of the West. _____

_____

_____

3. Many rodeo events lead to black eyes, broken ribs, dislocated shoulders, or even worse injuries. _____

_____

_____

4. Saddle-bronc riding, which requires coordination, balance, timing, is naturally considered the classic rodeo event. _____

_____

_____

5. The inmates of the Huntsville prison organize a well-publicized, rough-and-tumble rodeo every October. _____

_____

_____

As you read, watch for sentences that follow this pattern and add them below.

_____

_____

_____

_____

_____

_____

INVERSIONS

Not all sentences need to start with the traditional subject-verb combination. For variety you may want to invert the normal order and begin the sentence with a modifier out of its normal place; complements or direct objects may occasionally precede the subject. These inverted units may be single words, phrases, or dependent clauses.

Be careful when using this inverted pattern, however. It may lead to awkwardness. Inverting the natural order should always result in a graceful sentence, not one that seems forced or looks like a gimmick. Just as every sentence should seem natural, almost inevitable in its arrangement, the one that departs from traditional sentence order should be the same. Try not to call attention deliberately to any inversion; make it gracefully fit into the context. You want sentences that possess the magic of variety, yes; but remember that too much variety, too obviously achieved, may be worse than none at all. (See PATTERN 15a for further explanation.)

PATTERN 14:   PREPOSITIONAL PHRASE
                    BEFORE S AND V

Prepositional phrase   S   V   (or   V   S) .

Explanation

Before beginning this pattern, let's review what a preposition is. The name actually indicates its function: it has a "*pre*-position." The *pre* means that it comes before an object, which is necessary to make a prepositional phrase. For example, consider a box and a pencil. Where can you put the pencil in relation to the box? It might be "on the box" or "under the box," "beyond the box" or "near the box," "inside the box" or "beside the box."

In this pattern, you put one or more prepositional phrases at the beginning of the sentence. Make sure the modifying phrase does not sound awkward. Only your ear will tell you whether to put a comma after it; will the reader need the punctuation for each reading? If so, provide it.

For example, these sentences *must* have commas:

> After that, time had no meaning for him.
> Beyond this, Rex can probably never go.
> (Not "after that time" or "beyond this Rex.")

These sentences do well without a comma:

> Until next semester I have no more papers due.
> During the winter months Tom snowboards every day.

Examples

> After a long pause, the teacher continued.
>
> Despite his master's degree in world trade and economics, the only job David could get was making change in an Atlantic City casino.
>
> With horrified attention, we watched the planes crash into the World Trade Center.
>
> Under the table, Jenny played with her dolls.
>
> In the park the ducks waddled toward the pond.

Under the care of Bishop Jean Baptist Lamy, Sante Fe, New Mexico, became an important, thriving village.

On top of the desk, she put his CD player and his backpack.

Professional examples

"If you chart genealogy in a horizontal manner, you discover such curiosities as the fact that Jimmy Carter and Richard Nixon are sixth cousins."—*Everything Is Somewhere*

"When I left the dining room that evening and started down the dark basement stairs, I had a life."—Annie Dillard, "Hitting Pay Dirt"

"From the mist emerged a figure playing a flute."—*National Geographic*, August 1988

Checkpoint

✓ Sometimes a comma is necessary after the prepositional phrase, sometimes not. The sound and meaning of your sentence will guide you.

✓ A prepositional phrase can never stand alone. With no completion, it becomes a sentence fragment.

Exercises

In the following sentences, fill in the blanks. Some need prepositional phrases. In others, you need more words than a prepositional phrase to complete the sentence. Try to use *more* than one or two words in each blank.

1. To the athletes _____ , the new NCAA

   regulations represented _____ .

2. _____ stood the farmer holding a

   loaded shotgun.

3. After _____ yet before

   _____ , the veterans soon realized

   that _____ .

4. In _____ by

_____ of _____

_____ the Persian cat

_____ .

5. With a clear _____ of

the principles of _____ ,

a student _____ .

As you read, watch for sentences that follow this pattern and add them below.

_____

_____

_____

_____

_____

_____

_____

_____

> **PATTERN 15:**   OBJECT OR COMPLEMENT
>   BEFORE S AND V
>
> Object   or   Subject complement   S   V   .

Explanation

Occasionally you may wish to invert to stress some part of the sentence that ordinarily comes after the verb (the direct object or the subject complement). These usually go at the beginning of the sentence instead of in their normal positions. Any inversion adds invisible italics or stress. When you use PATTERN 15, always read your inversion aloud to be sure it sounds graceful in context, and that it blends well with the other sentences around it. Here, as in PATTERN 14, only the sound and rhythm of the sentence will tell you if you need a comma; there are no rules.

Examples

This example has the direct object before the subject-verb combination:

　　His kind of sarcasm I do not like.

These examples have a subject complement before the subject-verb combination:

　　SC   DO
　　Satisfied with his first draft, good grades he will never have.
　　No friend of snakes is my sister Jean.
　　Famous and wealthy an English professor will never be.

Professional examples

　　"Corded and crisp and pinafored, the five of us seated ourselves one by one at the counter."—Audre Lorde, "The Fourth of July"

　　"Up went the steps, bang went the door, round whirled the wheels, and off they rattled."—Charles Dickens, *The Old Curiosity Shop*

　　NOTE: Adverbs are stressed in this inversion.

Checkpoint

✓ Inversions are easy to do out of context, just for the exercise. But in a setting with other sentences, you need to take care that they sound natural, not forced or awkward. Use them sparingly, and then only for special emphasis.

Exercises

Supply the missing information in these inverted sentences:

1. _____ was Cinderella, but then neither were her stepsisters.

2. _____ a man sometimes loses his love.

3. _____ the Heisman Trophy may always be, yet it remains a goal of all college football players.

4. The Nobel Prize _____ _____ ; however, few _____ _____.

5. _____ electric cars might well become.

As you read, watch for sentences that follow this pattern and add them below.

_____

_____

_____

_____

_____

_____

_____

_____

PATTERN 15a:	COMPLETE INVERSION OF NORMAL PATTERN

Object *or* Complement *or* Modifier   V   S   .

Explanation

The standard English sentence goes

> subject—verb
>
> subject—verb—modifier
>
> subject—verb—completer (direct object or subject complement).

Completely reversing the order of these sentence parts creates an emphasis and a rhythm you cannot achieve in any other way:

> verb—subject
>
> modifier—verb—subject
>
> completer—verb—subject.

This pattern will add spice to your prose, but too many reversals, like too much garlic or cayenne pepper, can be overpowering. So don't overuse this pattern. It will probably fit better into dramatic statements or poetic prose passages than into business letters or laboratory reports.

Examples

Westward the country was free;	Mod S V C
westward, therefore, lay their hopes;	Mod V S
westward flew their dreams. The West became	Mod V S
for everyone the promised land of	Prep. phrase
milk and honey.	out of place
	between V
	and SC

From the guru's prophecy radiated a faith that ultimately all would be well.

Down the field and through the weeds pranced the little puppy.

In the writings of recent authors have we increasingly seen a sense of doom.

From his years of study came eventual understanding and compassion.

Young and beautiful the new CEO may be, but she has the credentials and skill to be effective.

Professional examples

"Never before have we had so little time to do so much."—Franklin Delano Roosevelt, "Fireside Chat," February 1942

"But craven he was not: sudden had been the call upon him and sudden was his answer to the call."—Thomas DeQuincey, "The English Mail Coach"

NOTE: The above sentence combines PATTERNS 15 and 15a.

Checkpoints

✓ Remember that this pattern should never offend the ear by sounding awkward or stilted.

✓ Test the sentence by reading it aloud. How does it sound? Is it consistent with your tone? Does it fit neatly into the context?

Exercises

Revise each of the following sentences so that you create a complete inversion of the normal subject-verb pattern. These may take some thought. You may have to add, delete, or alter some of the wording. The first one is done to give you an example.

1. The baseball player did not fear the pitcher. (Reworded: *Not fearing the pitcher, the baseball player strode confidently to the plate*).

2. When we go to Yosemite, I want to see El Capitan, Half Dome, and the falls. _____

   _____

3. Marching against the Mexican army, the brave Texans chanted, "Remember the Alamo!" _____

   _____

   _____

4. A human being's power of choice, either for good or evil, is boundless. _____

5. The dreamer and the doer live side by side in each of us. _____

_____

As you read, watch for sentences that follow this pattern and add them below.

_____

_____

_____

_____

_____

_____

_____

_____

_____

_____

AN ASSORTMENT OF PATTERNS

PATTERN 16:   PAIRED CONSTRUCTIONS

Not only ___ S ___ V ___ , but also ___ S ___ V ___ .

                                        (The *also* may be omitted.)

Just as ___ S ___ V ___ , so too ___ S ___ V ___ .

                                        (may be *so also* or simply *so*)

The more ___ S ___ V ___ , the more ___ S ___ V ___ .

                                        (may be *the less*)

The former ___ S ___ V ___ , the latter ___ S ___ V ___ .

If not ___ , at least ___ * ___ .

---

* Note that the *if not . . . at least* construction joins individual grammatical units, not complete clauses.

Explanation

Some words work in pairs; for example, *either* takes an *or; not only* takes *but also*. These are called *correlative conjunctions* and link words, phrases, or clauses that are similar in construction. The patterns in the box above illustrate some common phrases used for paired constructions that may occur in simple or in compound sentences. You will find these structures particularly helpful in making a comparison or a contrast.

    Whenever you use the last pattern, marked with an asterisk, remember to make both parts of the construction parallel. They both need the same grammatical structure and rhythm:

        Two nouns: if not *praise*, at least not *blame*

        Two prepositions: if not *in* the park, at least not *in* the back alley

        Two adjectives: if not *apple*, at least *pumpkin* pie

Examples

American tourists must realize that violations of laws in China are serious not only because they flaunt traditional codes of behavior but also because they reflect contempt for Oriental culture.

Just as the Yankees dominate the World Series, so Tiger Woods dominates the golf world.

Reluctantly, every dieter looks for a favorable verdict from the bathroom scale: if not a pound less, at least not an ounce more.

The more I study chemistry, the more confused I become.

The more he tried to please, the less pleased I was.

Kai and Ernst were two of my favorite ski instructors: the former taught me downhill racing; the latter helped carry me to the hospital where Dr. Alexander set my fractured arm.

Professional examples

"Not only do I knock them out, but I [also] pick the round."—Muhammad Ali

"It is not what they built, it is what they knocked down."—James Fenton, *German Requiem*

"Not only has the brush been kept in control but there's been an added benefit."—Edwin Kiester, Jr., *Smithsonian*, October 2001

"The more the critical reason dominates, the more impoverished life becomes."—Carl Jung

"Americans saw it [Faulkner's speech] not as a message directed only to writers and artists but [also] as an appeal to all."—*Harper Book of American Quotations*

Checkpoints

✓ Remember that pair means "two." Be sure to supply the second part of the construction; don't give the reader a signal suggesting two items and then provide only one. To say "Not only is she pretty" and then say no more leaves your reader confused.

MORE PAIRS: The following correlative conjunctions may help you in developing this pattern:

whether . . . or	*so . . . that*
such . . . that	*not only . . . more than that*
both . . . and	*as . . . as*
neither . . . nor	*not so . . . as*

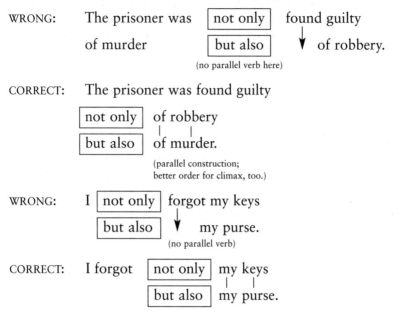

CAUTION: Put both conjunctions of a pair in logical places so that what follows each one will be parallel.

WRONG: The prisoner was │ not only │ found guilty
           of murder │ but also │ ↓ of robbery.
                      (no parallel verb here)

CORRECT: The prisoner was found guilty
           │ not only │ of robbery
           │ but also │ of murder.
                      (parallel construction;
                      better order for climax, too.)

WRONG: I │ not only │ forgot my keys
           │ but also │ ↓ my purse.
                      (no parallel verb)

CORRECT: I forgot │ not only │ my keys
           │ but also │ my purse.

Exercises

Complete the following sentences with logically paired constructions:

1. The _____ Robert tried to please

   his fiancee, the _____ dissatisfied

   _____ .

2. The _____ a teenager tries

   to rebel, the _____

   parents _____

   _____ .

3. Just as video games can be entertaining _____

   _____ , so

   _____ .

4. The Jaguar's beauty is _____

_____ in its design _____

_____ in its function.

5. _____ if not the

ice cream, at least the birthday cake.

Correct the following errors in parallelism:

1. Robert not only forgot to bring the wine to the party but also the ice.

_____

_____

_____

2. His father-in-law offered John nothing, neither a position with the

brokerage firm nor a monthly allowance. _____

_____

_____

3. During the wedding ceremony the spectators smiled both at their

friends and relatives and the flower girl, who proudly carried her

basket. _____

_____

_____

As you read, watch for sentences that follow this pattern and add them below.

_____

_____

_____

_____

_____

_____

_____

_____

_____

_____

PATTERN 16a: A PAIRED CONSTRUCTION
FOR CONTRAST ONLY

A "*this*, not *that*" or "*not this*, but *that*" construction _____ .

in some place other than the verb position

Explanation

This type of paired construction—the simple contrast—illustrates the differences between two ideas and usually involves a reversal. This reversal may be dramatically emphatic or may simply reinforce an ironic purpose. Unlike PATTERN 16, this one does *not* involve correlative conjunctions. To show a reversal in the middle of your statement, simply say something is "*this*, not *that*" or "*not this*, but *that*." Punctuation marks—especially commas, dashes, or parentheses—will help indicate a break in your sentence and establish your point of reversal or contrast.

Examples

For some hummingbirds, migration involves a much smaller range, measured in hundreds, not thousands, of miles.

By chance (not by studying) she made an A on the midterm.

The famous actor was convinced that it was his personality, not his money, that attracted women.

Hard work, not luck, gets you promoted in business.

For many people, now, it is football—not baseball—that is the National Pastime.

The judge asked for acquittal—not conviction.

Professional examples

I believe that man will not merely endure; he will prevail."— William Faulkner, Nobel Prize Speech, Stockholm, Sweden

"Custer raises his saber no longer (the 7th Cavalry didn't carry sabers into battle); his hair doesn't flow in the hot wind (he had cut off his hair, and there was not even a breeze that day); nor is he clad all in buckskins (he had stripped off his jacket in the heat); nor is he standing (not if they shot him in the ribs by the river); nor do the Sioux race around him on their horses (most were dismounted); nor do they charge him with war clubs (most were sensibly shooting their bows and rifles from distant tangles of sage)."—Andrew Ward, "The Little Bighorn," *American Heritage*, April 1992

> NOTE: This sentence, a variation of PATTERN 11a, states various misconceptions about General Custer and the Sioux, then debunks them with the information in parentheses.

"Life is not a spectacle or a feast; it is a predicament."—George Santayana

"When we are happy we are always good, but when we are good we are not always happy."—Oscar Wilde

Exercises

Using the following sentences for words and ideas, create contrasting "*this*, not *that*" or "*not this*, but *that*" sentences. Use dashes and parentheses as well as commas to establish your point of reversal.

1. Saddle-bronc riding is the classic rodeo event even though many spectators prefer the dangerous Brahma-bull-riding contests. _____

   _____

   _____

   _____

2. Although Dennis said he could swim, he would not go into the water

   _____

   _____

   _____ .

3. With horror Sandra realized that Jerrell was a werewolf; he had been masquerading as a royal prince of Transylvania. _____

   _____

   _____

Create complete sentences, using for each one the indicated point of contrast.

1. _____ —not

   romance— _____ .

2. _____ , not freedom.

3. _____ (not just

   milk and a sandwich) _____

   _____ .

Create a point of contrast for each of the following incomplete structures:

1. The trip turned out to be a disaster—not _____

   _____ .

2. My friend could wear casual clothes, but not _____

   _____ .

3. No _____ , Ashley tripped

   and spilled her drink.

4. The audience did not want the musicians to stop; _____

   _____ .

5. A preacher wants to save his members, not merely _____

   _____ .

As you read, watch for sentences that follow this pattern and add them below.

PATTERN 17:   DEPENDENT CLAUSE
                   (in a "sentence slot")
                   AS SUBJECT OR OBJECT
                   OR COMPLEMENT

S [dependent clause as subject]   V   .

S   V   [dependent clause as object or complement] .

Explanation

As you learn to vary your sentence structures, alternating simple with more complex ones, this pattern can be especially helpful in achieving variety and style. Although a sophisticated pattern, it is (strangely enough) quite common in speech; it is easy to use in your written work, too, if you understand that the dependent clause is merely a part (subject, object, or complement) of the independent clause.

The dependent clauses in this pattern, which serve as nouns, will begin with one of the following words:

who, whom, which, that, what, why, where, when, how

then come the subject-verb of the dependent clause. If one of these introductory words IS the subject, it will need only a verb after it.

Examples

[*How he did that*] is still amazing to me.

(subject of verb *is*)

He finally finished [*what he had started over a year ago.*]

(complement after *finished*)

[*What man cannot imagine*], he cannot create.

(object of *can create* in this "inverted" sentence)

Ann never discovered [*why her husband bought her a diamond necklace*].

(object of verb *discovered*)

[*Why so many people hate to eat vegetables*] constantly amazes parents and nutritionists.

(subject of *amazes*)

[*Who assassinated President Kennedy*] continues to be a hotly debated subject.

(introductory phrase is subject)

[*That he was a werewolf*] became obvious when his fingernails turned into claws.

(subject of verb *became*)

Professional examples

"And so my fellow Americans, ask not

[what your country can do for you];

[clause as DO]

ask [what you can do for your country]."—John F. Kennedy

[clause as OBJ of prep. *for*]

"A somewhat sweet red meat [that tastes like venison], kangaroo is usually served medium rare or rare."—*MM* Magazine, December 2001

[clause as SC]

"He, O men, [who like Socrates], knows that his wisdom is in truth worth nothing."—Plato, *Apology*

[clause as SC]

"The world itself, [whose single meaning I do not understand], is a vast irrational."—Albert Camus

[clause as SC]

Checkpoint

✓ Remember—the dependent clause can never stand alone; it is only a portion of your sentence. Don't put a period before or after it because you will create an awkward fragment, as in these two examples:

With horror she realized that he was a philanderer. Why her mother had a low opinion of him.

Juliet never realizes why her decision to drink the sleeping potion is irrational. Which explains why she drinks it.

How would you correct these errors?

Exercises

Revise the following sentences. Some need to be completed with an independent clause. Others need a dependent clause.

1. After many years of research the scientist realized that _____

_____ .

2. Why _____ worried

her sisters and brothers.

3. What runners _____

_____ , they can usually manage.

4. That _____

became easier for me to understand after I thought about it.

5. How often she _____

_____ shocked not only _____

_____ but also _____

_____ .

As you read, watch for sentences that follow this pattern and add them below.

_____

_____

_____

_____

_____

_____

_____

_____

_____

_____

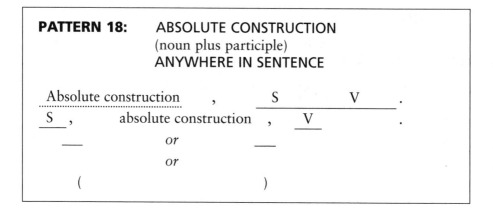

Explanation

This pattern stands out because it does not resemble anything else in English grammar. An absolute construction uses a noun or pronoun plus a participle and has no grammatical connection to the rest of the sentence. It does explain or elaborate on the sentence.

The participle—a verb form but not a verb—can be present, ending in –*ing*; past, ending in –*d* or –*ed*; or irregular, such as *torn* or *slept*.

With present participles:

The American economy, God willing, will soon return to normal.

With past participles:

The old man, prejudiced by past experience, viewed the newcomer with distrust.

With irregular participles (*torn* and *burnt* here):

Her skirt torn and her leg burnt, Sara cried on her mother's shoulder after the accident.

If you wish, you may even use several participles and then contradict all of them with a contrasting adjective, as the following sentence illustrates:

Caesar continued his march through Gaul, his army tattered, exhausted, hardened—but victorious.

These constructions are not dependent clauses because they don't contain a verb and, for the same reason, are not independent clauses: if you leave the phrase out, the sentence is still clear.

ABSOLUTE:	His ball being lost, Johnny had to quit playing tennis for the day.
DEPENDENT CLAUSE:	Because his ball was lost, Johnny had to quit playing tennis for the day.
INDEPENDENT CLAUSE:	His ball was lost, so Johnny had to quit playing tennis for the day.

This pattern can give added variety to your writing. However, if you merely toss it in, it can become awkward. Don't force it, but do look for places where this pattern will enhance your writing naturally.

Examples

The walls being blank, the new tenant—an unemployed artist—promptly set about covering all of them in a mural of orange, vermillion, and yellow.

I want to go away to college (my parents willing) as soon as I graduate from high school.

The snow having stopped, we were able to continue our journey.

The audience bored, many began to go to sleep.

Professional examples

"She sat back on the bed, her head bowed, her lips moving feverishly, her eyes rising only to scan the walls."—Anne Rice, *Interview with the Vampire*

"Douglas Camps's *Small Iriabo,* for example—fashioned of steel, copper and wood and finished with red paint—represents a young Kalabari Ijo girl".—*Smithsonian,* October 2001

Checkpoint

✓ The absolute construction, because it has no grammatical connection with the sentence, must always have some punctuation. Use a comma if it comes at the beginning of the sentence or before one at the end. If it comes in the middle of the sentence, enclose it with a pair of commas, dashes, or parentheses.

Exercises

Provide an absolute construction for the blank in each of the following sentences:

1. The fabulous paintings in the Prado thrilled me, all of them _____

   _____ .

2. The lion tamer entered the cage, his demeanor _____

   _____ .

3. Their faces _____ , the ice

   skaters _____ .

4. The sounds of the airport—jets _____

   _____ , people _____ , the

   public address system _____—suggest

   the excitement, frustration, and chaos of the place.

5. The guitarist's hands moved over the strings, his right hand _____

   _____ , his left hand _____

   _____ .

As you read, watch for sentences that follow this pattern and add them
below.

_____

_____

_____

_____

_____

_____

_____

_____

_____

PATTERN 19:	THE SHORT, SIMPLE SENTENCE FOR RELIEF OR DRAMATIC EFFECT

$$\underline{\qquad\qquad S \qquad\qquad V \qquad} .$$

Explanation

This pattern can provide intense clarity, but being brief alone will not make it dramatic. Actually, this pattern will be effective only

> when you use it after several long sentences, or
>
> when you let it more or less summarize what you have just said, or
>
> when you let it provide transition between two or more ideas.

Although "All was lost." or "Thus it ended." may not look very startling here, in the appropriate context such a sentence may be quite dramatic. After a series of long, involved sentences, a short statement will grab the readers' attention, make them pause, shock them into considering the ideas in the longer sentences that precede it.

As you develop your style, your ear will hear "a good turn of phrase" and you will be able to use this pattern effectively.

Polonius knew this.

Examples

Well, I wonder.	But then it happened.
Days passed.	Just consider this.
It was magical.	Don't laugh.
That is not my style.	That is okay.
Perseverance pays.	I think not.
It is time to move on.	And this is true.
All efforts failed.	He was unbeatable.
Everything changed.	Let's talk.

Professional examples

"Jesus wept."—The Bible

"The buck stops here."—sign on Harry Truman's desk

"Know thyself."—Plutarch, *Lives*

"Make my day."—Clint Eastwood in *Dirty Harry*

"I came, I saw, I conquered."—Julius Caesar

"Call me Ishmael." (the dramatic first sentence in *Moby Dick*)

NOTE: Try to imagine the context that would make these sentences dramatic and effective. Some experienced writers, such as Charles Dickens, join a number of short, balanced thoughts into one long sentence that could have been broken down into a series of short sentences, brief and dramatic. But imagine how choppy the opening of *A Tale of Two Cities* would have sounded if Dickens had used short sentences rather than one long sentence, with a series of parallel and balanced parts:

"It was the best of times, it was the worst of times, it was the age of wisdom, it was the age of foolishness, it was the epoch of belief, it was the epoch of incredulity, it was the season of Light, it was the season of Darkness, it was the spring of hope, it was the winter of despair, we had everything before us, we had nothing before us, we were all going direct to Heaven, we were all going direct the other way—in short, the period was so far like the present period, that some of its noisiest authorities insisted on its being received, for good or for evil, in the superlative degree of comparison only."—Charles Dickens, *A Tale of Two Cities*

Checkpoints

✓ Sentences such as "I like petunias." or "Children laugh." don't fit this pattern just because they are short. They might, of course, but only in the proper context.

✓ Notice how professional writers employ this technique of short sentences for special effects.

✓ This pattern works best when it is emphatic, points up a contrast, or summarizes dramatically.

PATTERN 19a: A SHORT QUESTION
FOR DRAMATIC EFFECT

(Interrogative word) auxiliary verb   S   V   ?

(Interrogative word standing alone)   ?

(Question based solely on intonation)   ?

Auxiliary verb   S   V   ?

Explanation

This pattern involves either of two basic constructions: a question that begins with an interrogative word, or a statement that becomes a question through intonation (pitch or tone) of voice.

It is effective in several places:

in the introduction to arouse the reader's interest;

as a topic sentence to introduce a paragraph;

within the paragraph to provide variety;

between paragraphs to provide transition;

at the end to provide a thought-provoking conclusion.

When you write, look in these five places to discover where a question could serve some desired effect. You can provoke your readers with staccato-like questions, wake them up, make them pause and think, or make them ask *why* about your subject.

Examples

Can we change?   How did she cope?

Why do it?   What is next?

Where to now?   What if E.T. calls?

Was it easy?   When will it end?

The following examples suggested by intonation are more common in conversation than in formal prose. Imagine how the voice rises at the end of each question.

That's her mother?

You made an *A* in Esch's class?

James flunked modern dance?

Remember typewriters?

Professional examples

"What price glory?"—Maxwell Anderson

"Is sex dirty?"—Woody Allen

"Are we having fun yet?"—Zippy the Pinhead

Checkpoints

✓ Questions need to be handled carefully to be effective.

✓ Avoid scattering them around just because they are easy; make them serve some purpose, such as to arouse curiosity, to stimulate interest, to lead the reader into some specific idea about your subject.

Exercises

In what you are reading, look for the short, dramatic question. Copy the sentence here and add a comment about its function within the overall context; recall that there are at least five effects, and try to find an example of each.

1. Example: _____

_____

   Comment: _____

_____

2. Example: _____

_____

   Comment: _____

_____

3. Example: _____

_____

Comment: _____

_____

4. Example: _____

_____

Comment: _____

_____

5. Example: _____

_____

Comment: _____

_____

PATTERN 20:   THE DELIBERATE FRAGMENT

Merely a part of a sentence

Explanation

The mention of a fragment makes some teachers reach for their red pen. Good writers, ironically enough, often use fragments for emphasis or to create a dramatic effect. A deliberate fragment should serve some special purpose; if it doesn't, don't use it. Used sparingly, a fragment, like the short sentence or short question in PATTERN 19, can be very effective. Overused, it becomes just a gimmick.

Examples

Here are some effective fragments:

1. in a description—

> I wish you could have known the Southwest in the early days. The way it really was. The way the land seemed to reach out forever. And those endless stretches of blue sky! The incredible clarity of air which made distance an illusion. I wish I could make you see it so you would understand my nostalgia—nostalgia and sorrow for a wonder that is no more.

2. for transition—

> Now, on with the story.
>
> But to get back to the subject.
>
> So much for that.
>
> Next? The crucial question to be answered.
>
> First, the nuts and bolts.
>
> Meanwhile.

3. for indicating conclusions—

> Fair enough.   All too late.
>
> No matter.   Fine.

4. in structuring a question or an answer—

> But how?
>
> And why not?
>
> What then? Nothing.
>
> Based on logic? Hardly!
>
> Where and when and why?

5. for making exclamations and for emphasis—

> What a price to pay!
>
> Probably not!
>
> Never!
>
> The next step—martyrdom.
>
> Shameful nonsense.

6. for making explanations—

> All to no avail.
>
> But for short journeys.

7. and sometimes in aphorisms or fragments of clichés—

> The more the merrier for them, too.
>
> But there's the rub.
>
> Early to bed!
>
> Absolute power corrupting once more.

Professional examples

> "From bebop to hip-hop—the fast-talkin', ribs-smackin', spraygun-of-the-world Quincy Jones."—*MM* Magazine, December 2001

> "Adults of a certain age and late night viewers everywhere know the rest. How the masked man brought peace and goodwill to the Old West."—David H. Shayt, *Smithsonian,* December 2001

Checkpoints

✓ If you are in the habit of writing fragments, don't think you have mastered this pattern!

✓ Use this pattern, like PATTERNS 19 and 19a, only as a deliberate styling device. It should never be merely an accident or a mistake in sentence structure or punctuation.

CAUTION: Use PATTERNS 19, 19a, and 20 sparingly and precisely.

Exercises

In your reading look for highly styled, deliberate fragments used for dramatic effect. Copy the fragment and add a brief comment about its function or purpose.

1. Example: _____

_____

Comment: _____

_____

2. Example: _____

_____

Comment: _____

_____

3. Example: _____

_____

Comment: _____

_____

4. Example: _____

_____

Comment: _____

_____

5. Example: _____

_____

Comment: _____

_____

CHAPTER 3

Sentences Grow

STYLE

As we have shown, sentence variety can significantly enhance your writing. In this section we look at ways to combine the patterns for even greater effectiveness.

First, these few tips will make your writing more interesting and livelier.

1. Avoid the use of "to be" verbs (*am, are, is, was, were*). Although useful, they show no action and their overuse will make your writing boring.

   WEAK: Kim Nelson is my English teacher. She is a very good teacher.
   BETTER: Kim Nelson, my English teacher, makes our class special.

2. Many of these "to be" problems become worse when used in expletive sentences—sentences that begin with "There is," "There are," "It is," and so on. Since the subject of the sentence is delayed, a reader may lose interest. These sentences also lead to wordiness.

   WEAK: There is a man who lives next door to me who has a mean dog.
   BETTER: My neighbor has a mean dog.

3. The strength of a sentence lies in the verbs. The more exact your verb choice, the more graphic and forceful your sentence will be.

   WEAK: The teacher walked slowly into the room.
   BETTER: The teacher ambled (or strolled) into the room.

These few tips, incorporated into the sentence patterns you have already learned, will allow your writing to better hold the reader's interest.

   NOTE: For more on style, see *On Writing Well* by William Zinsser. Harper, 2001.

Now you are ready to make sentences grow . . . and grow some more.

You are now familiar with some of the more complex patterns in CHAPTER 2, so let's combine two or more of them to create additional variety. Only a few examples of sentence combinations appear in this chapter, but you will discover many more possibilities as you experiment on your own. Remember these cautions, however: Always try to write a sentence that fits into the total context; never force a construction simply for the sake of variety.

Don't be afraid to be creative. Experiment not only with your own favorite patterns from CHAPTER 2 but also with others, with new ones you will discover in your reading or create in your own writing. When you learn to maneuver sentence patterns, when you feel at ease manipulating words, then you will be a master of sentence structure.

Now to discover what patterns combine well—

COMBINING THE PATTERNS—TEN WAYS

1. The compound sentence with a colon combines effectively with a series and the repetition of a key term (PATTERNS 3, 4, 9a).

   > To the Victorians much in life was sacred: Marriage was sacred, the family circle was sacred, society was sacred, the British Empire was sacred.

2. Repetition also combines well with a dependent clause as an interrupting modifier (PATTERNS 9, 11).

   > The experiences of the past—because they are experiences of the past—too seldom guide our actions today.

3. A dependent clause as complement combines well with an appositive at the end of a sentence after a colon and a series with balanced pairs (PATTERNS 17, 10, 5).

   > Ted became what he had long aspired to be: a master of magic and illusion, of hypnotism and sleight-of-hand tricks.

4. The series without a conjunction and the repetition of a key term combine well with the introductory appositive and an inversion of any kind (PATTERNS 4, 9, 9a, 15a).

   > The generation that was too young to remember a depression, too young to remember World War II, too young even to vote—from that generation came America's soldiers for Southeast Asia.

5. The compound sentence without a conjunction can combine with repetitions and series (PATTERNS 1, 4, 4a, 9).

> Books of elegiac poetry had always stirred Jason; they made him think of music, music that sang of ancient glories, of brave men, of the things they loved and hated and died for.

6. Introductory appositives may be written as dependent clauses and the repetition of a key term may be followed by a question for dramatic effect (PATTERNS 6, 8, 9, 19a).

> That there are too many people, that overcrowding causes social, economic, and political problems, that human fellowship and compassion wear thin in such an environment— these are problems facing the inner city today, problems that eventually young people must solve. But how will they?

7. An inversion of the sentence pattern may also include a prepositional phrase before the subject-verb combination within a compound sentence (PATTERNS 1, 14, 15a).

> Around Jay were men of various nationalities; to none of them could he ever really relate.

8. A pair of dependent clauses as direct objects will work well with paired words, a series without a conjunction, an interrupting modifier with dashes, and a repetition of the same word in a parallel construction (PATTERNS 4, 11, 9a, 16, 17).

> The ambassador found that not only was America experiencing painful expansion and costly social upheavals—over foreign policy, racial disorder, economic priorities—but also that the nation was facing the threat of a national paralysis of will, a paralysis of faith.

9. An interrupting modifier that is itself a sentence may go well with another type of modifier (PATTERNS 11, 11a).

> His family, a respected conservative family ruled mainly by several maiden aunts—his father had died when he was a child—had been scandalized at the thought that their young heir wanted to devote his entire life to hot-rod racing and roller-derby competition.

10. After a long, involved compound sentence without a conjunction, a fragment with a repeated key word and then a fragmentary question may be very effective (PATTERNS 1, 4a, 9a, 20).

> The ecology-awareness movement aims at balance and wholeness and health in our environment; it wants to assure a proper place in the scheme of things for people, for plants,

and for animals. Not an exclusive place for either one, just a proper place for each. But how?

Sentences for analysis

The following sentences from professional writers combine several patterns you learned in CHAPTER 2. Identify them, looking for their special characteristics. Pay particular attention to series structures, length, balance, the amount and appropriateness of detail, effective punctuation, and the appearance of sentences within other sentences. More important, look for patterns that you can adapt to your own style.

1. The 190E Mercedes Benz is a car to respect, to value, to appreciate; the 500SL is a car to adore.

----

2. See how the writer has used an out-of-breath repetition at the end of this sentence. Notice that it contains an allusion to Bugsy Siegel, one of the early developers of Las Vegas.

   "The lights rippled, rolled, darted, sequenced their way through fantastical patterns against the black, empty screen of beyond, millions and millions of lights, more than crazy Bugsy could have imagined, far more than someone who's never spent a night in Las Vegas could ever, ever, ever—even in the wildest reaches of dreams —hope to comprehend."—Kathryn Marshall, *American Way,* September 1991

----

3. "Everything for which Japan is known exists in Kyoto: The modern rush and bother and sex and sleaze and chrome and high-technology excitement are all there; but alongside the finest and most exquisite food, the most classical and revered exponents and teachers of various schools of tea ceremony, of flower arranging, of kabuke and noh, the most renowned teachings of the art of the geisha, the best in damascene, lacquer, in handmade paper, in dolls, the art of sand raking, of potting, of making brocades, of arranging the Kimono, of fashioning tiny gardens with moss, of diverting small streams— in short, everything, for those of an alliterative bent, from Zen to

Zaitech."—Simon Winchester, "Kyoto," *Condé Nast Traveler,*
February 1992

---

4. "Imagine a macadam track from San Francisco to Wichita, barely
   two lanes wide with no markings on most stretches, serving the
   following traffic: ten-ton trucks constantly jockeying to pass one
   another, buses with riders hanging on for their lives, big cars called
   Ambassadors that lumber along like tanks, camel trains, oxcarts,
   cycle rickshaws, wandering cows, motor scooters, bicycles and
   pedestrians, including the occasional itinerant with a dancing bear on
   a leash."—Constance Bond, *Smithsonian,* May 1992

---

5. "Here is an 1872 brochure for weather vanes: horses, roosters, cows,
   eagles, plows, fish, hogs, swans, cannon, shovels, flags, peacocks,
   stars."—*Smithsonian,* April 1991

---

6. "After the Lincoln County War [New Mexico in 1878], Billy [the
   Kid] failed to live up to his potential—not as a respectable, law-
   abiding citizen, not as a Robin Hood battling against injustice, not
   as a cold-blooded killer, not even as the premier outlaw of all
   time."—Robert Utley, "Billy the Kid Country," *American Heritage,*
   April 1991

---

7. Writing in the *Washington Post,* Henry Allen raised press bashing to
   a level rarely heard since [Gen. William T.] Sherman: "The Persian
   Gulf press briefings are making reporters look like fools, nitpickers
   and egomaniacs; like dilettantes who have spent exactly none of their
   lives on the end of a gun or even a shovel; dinner party commandos,
   slouching inquisitors, collegiate spitball artists; people who have
   never been in a fistfight much less combat; a whining, self-righteous,

upper-middle-class mob jostling for whatever tiny flakes of fame may settle on their shoulders like some sort of Pulitzer Prize dandruff."
—Peter Andrews, "The Media and the Military," *American Heritage,*
July–August 1991

---

8. "American families in shorts, bickering and road-weary, climb and descend the macadam path to Last Stand Hill, the women stumping along with their aim-and-shoots, the children fidgeting with their Nintendo Gameboys, the men in caps explaining with the instant authority of sports fans—'Now listen to me, kids'—that the marble stones that punctuate the battlefield mark where the troopers are buried (they don't exactly), that the fighting was hand to hand (it wasn't), that the Sioux tricked Custer (they didn't), that he is buried beneath the monument on Custer Hill (if he is, it's inadvertent; he's supposed to be buried at West Point, but some believe that in 1877 a burial detail may have shipped the wrong set of disinterred remains, in which case an enlisted man has been impersonating an officer for more than a century)."—Andrew Ward, "The Little Bighorn," *American Heritage,* April 1992

---

9. "It [the maze] has been used for courting (a favorite place for Tudor trysts); for religious processions (the line of worshippers never once crossing); as a form of contemplation and penance (monks supposedly shuffling along the stony paths on their knees); and, even now, for fertility rites—a gameskeeper in Hampshire is always having to move couples on from one particular maze site."—Martin O'Brien, "Garden-Variety Puzzles," *Travel and Life*

---

10. "Whether the Southwest will develop a distinct culture I do not know. I only know that if a distinctly Southwestern culture is developed, it will employ cattle brands and no signs of the zodiac to ornament the facades of its buildings; that its gardens will be made

beautiful by native mountain laurel as well as by English boxwood; that it will paint with the colors of the Painted Desert as well as with the colors of the Aegean; that is, biographers will have to understand Sam Houston better than they understand John Quincy Adams; that is, actors on the stage will cultivate the drawl of the old-time Texans rather than the broad *a*'s of Boston; and that the aroma of jasmine and bluebonnets, the golden fragility of the *retama,* the sting of a dry norther, the lonely howl of the coyote, and the pulsing silence of places where machines do not murder quietude—such things will appeal to the senses through the rhythems [*sic*] of its poets."
—J. Frank Dobie, quoted in Clark Kimball, *The Southwest Printer,* Texas Western Press, 1990

EXPANDING SENTENCES

Often writers need more than a simple sentence with only a noun and a verb. Modifiers help illustrate the generalization of the main sentence. To make their meaning clearer, writers add one or more modifiers to help explain, describe, or amplify so the sentence will be more meaningful to the reader. Modifiers can be placed anywhere in the sentence. Francis Christensen, *Notes Toward a New Rhetoric* (New York: Harper and Row, 1967), named this type of expanded sentence the "cumulative sentence." In it the base sentence of main subject and main verb with their "bound modifiers" (those that cannot move about) *accumulates* additions. To the base one adds "free modifiers" (those that can move about) that enrich the sentence and create a feeling of motion. A later description of the Christensen method appears in *A New Rhetoric* (New York: Harper and Row, 1976).

The primary sentence is the first level and the modifiers are the second, third, or even fourth level. Each level needs to be connected to the one immediately above it and is related to the basic sentence.

Study the examples that follow and notice how modifiers on different levels in the subject slot help expand the sentence and clarify its meaning.

LEVEL ONE: the basic slots for any sentence (S—V)

Whooping cranes fly. (the "kernel sentence," according to Francis Christensen)

Now, on different levels add modifiers to the subject.

LEVEL TWO: (the first modifiers): may come before or after subject or verb:

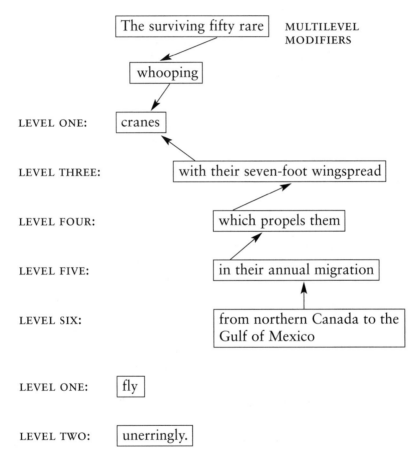

LEVEL ONE: fly

LEVEL TWO: unerringly.

Now add more modifiers on different levels in the verb slot:

LEVEL ONE (the basic S—V): <u>Whooping</u> <u>cranes</u> <u>fly</u>.

LEVEL TWO: modifiers for the verb:

> unerringly and swiftly overhead

LEVEL TWO EXPANDED (more modifiers for the verb):

> as they migrate southward

LEVEL THREE: modifier for some part of *that* modifier

> using a kind of built-in radar

LEVEL FOUR: more modifiers with more modifiers

> in their search

> for winter quarters

> near Aransas Pass.

Now see what modifiers can do to a basic sentence:

> The surviving fifty rare whooping cranes, with their seven-foot wingspread, which propels them in their annual migration from northern Canada to the Gulf of Mexico, fly unerringly and swiftly overhead as they migrate southward using a kind of built-in radar in their search for winter quarters near Aransas Pass.

MYTHS ABOUT COORDINATORS

Some writers believe you should not begin a sentence with one of the FANBOYS—the seven coordinators: *for, and, nor, but, or, yet, so.* Nevertheless, many experienced writers *do* use coordinators now and then to begin sentences and to link ideas. Review the coordinators and their meanings; then observe how professional writers use them effectively to begin sentences.

for Gives a reason why something did or did not occur. There is a causal connection between two thoughts.

and Adds to the information previously given, implying continuation of a thought.

nor Continues a previous negative thought.

but Signals an exception, or something contrary to the first thought. *But* implies opposition or contrast in a causal way.

or Gives an alternative, another opinion. *Or* suggests only one alternative at a time.

yet Implies a conditional situation; something true despite apparent obstacles.

so Shows a consequence, a result, or a reason for something to occur.

Examples

For we had to leave early.
For it was magical.
For the champion was unbeatable.
And now you can finish the assignment.
And in the middle of that Stones tune, too.
Nor did she give a reason.
Nor can I explain.
But peace of mind remains as elusive as ever.
But he, too, helped with the rescue.
Or you could take an earlier flight and arrive in Honolulu about 4:15 P.M.
Or you can take an alternative route and avoid the traffic.
Yet few remember him.
Yet we find exceptions to this pattern.
So we finally got to go.
So that's it.
So we'll start here.

Professional examples

"And that's the way it is."—Walter Cronkite, CBS Evening News sign-off line

NOTE: The quote above is the final line of a long article.

"But now I'm a big boy too and I can do anything and anything and anything."—Ernest Hemingway, *The Garden of Eden*

Exercises

As you read, observe how professional writers often use the short, simple sentence for dramatic effect. Copy the sentence here and add a comment about its function in the overall context—to provide transition, to give variety, to shock the reader, and so on.

1. Example: _____

   _____

   Comment: _____

   _____

2. Example: _____

   _____

   Comment: _____

   _____

3. Example: _____

   _____

   Comment: _____

   _____

4. Example: _____

   _____

   Comment: _____

   _____

5. Example: _____

   _____

   Comment: _____

   _____

A SENTENCE WITH SPECIAL EMPHASIS:
THE PERIODIC SENTENCE

A special pattern that helps create suspense is the *periodic sentence.* Unlike the *loose* or *cumulative sentence,* which begins with the main clause and continues with supporting details, the periodic sentence delays statements of the central idea until the period at the end. The important thought is deliberately withheld from the reader to create a special climax.

Every sentence has points where you place known and unknown information. In other words, your reader will be looking in particular places for something new. Sometimes you may delay giving this unknown information until the end of the sentence, the primary point of emphasis. A periodic sentence enables you to place the unknown at a strategically powerful point.

A second point of emphasis is near the beginning, in the subject slot. Here, you place known information, because it is not so crucial as what is new. If you bury new information in the middle, it will be forgotten.

You won't use many periodic sentences. In fact, the majority will be loosely structured. Sometimes, though, you will want to withhold unfamiliar information to create suspense. Place the less important items first, then gradually move toward the more important, with the most vital bit saved for a climactic ending. This humorous sentence illustrates the periodic structure: "I attribute such success as I have had to the use of the periodic sentence."

Now analyze this example:

> "While caravan after caravan winds its weary way across the desert sands, bringing precious cargo from far inland marts to the bazaars that are the meeting-places of the East and West, most of the camels in these trains announce their coming through the melodious tinkling of brass bells."—Brochure on camel bells of Sarna

How did the writer create suspense? What crucial bit of information was withheld until the very end? What is the purpose of the details in the long clause that begins the sentence?

Now contrast the loose structure of the first sentence below with the periodic structure of the second:

> If the voters pass the measure, the new park will be built downtown.

> The new park will be built downtown, if the voters pass the measure.

Sentences for analysis

Analyze these periodic sentences. Remember the characteristics of the pattern.

1. "From the deserts of Arizona to the Baltic coastline of Sweden; from Italy to India; from Chile to Celtic Britain; from wavering Bronze Age rock carvings and medieval stone-and-turf designs to the more recent and the more formal garden variety built of evergreens such as yew and holly, the pattern of the maze has appeared throughout history with mystifying regularity in a score of unrelated cultures."—Martin O'Brien, "Garden-Variety Puzzles," *Travel and Life*

2. "Sketch a simple picture of azure waters, gentle breezes, and a protected anchorage; add a wash of tropical sunset colors—and you have a portrait of Cruz Bay."—Kenneth Brower, *National Geographic Traveler,* September/October 1992

3. "She never gives up. Her blue hair waved, circles of rouge on her wrinkled cheeks, lipstick etching the lines around her mouth, still moisturizing her skin nightly, still corseted, she dies."—Una Stannard, "The Mask of Beauty," *A Woman's Place*

4. "From Stettin in the Baltic to Trieste in the Adriatic, an iron curtain has descended across the continent."—Winston Churchill, Westminster College, Fulton, Missouri, March 1946

CHAPTER 4

Figurative Language in Sentences

Figurative language uses devices to expand meaning. It cannot be taken literally. It departs from conventional use to produce a special effect, often emotional. You need to be careful to avoid clichés (worn-out or too familiar phrases), which will detract from your effectiveness. Here is a brief discussion of the more common figures of speech.

FIGURES OF SPEECH

Allusion

Allusion is another way of making a comparison; it suggests a similarity between what you are writing about and something that your reader has read before or heard about. The success of the allusion, of course, will depend on whether you strike a responsive chord and your reader recognizes it.

Allusions, richly connotative or symbolic, always suggest more than the words say. Because they add so much, your readers will gain depth of meaning.

If you want to allude to something, let a word, phrase, or even your very style suggest a similarity between the subject and some other idea, a similarity real or imaginary. Choose allusions that will fit your audience as well as the context of your paper.

Remember that obscure allusions will cloud communication, but appropriate ones will enable you to say more in fewer words.

Common referents are history, the Bible, mythology, literature, popular personalities. In fact, a whole group of words entered the language first as allusions to persons well known in life or literature: a political maverick, a boycott, sandwiches, the little Corsican, a Mae West life jacket, an Achilles heel. How many allusions can you find in popular advertising? Or in book titles? Or in popular music?

Grapes of Wrath and *East of Eden* (both allude to the Bible)

Tender Is the Night (alludes to Keats's nightingale ode)

The Sun Also Rises (alludes to *Ecclesiastes*)

Leave Her to Heaven (alludes to *Hamlet*)

Wonderland (alludes to *Alice in Wonderland*)

Can you add other titles to the list?

Examples

Even if you have miles to go, you should never abandon a project without finishing it. (alludes to Robert Frost's "Stopping by Woods on a Snowy Evening")

He needed the Force to help him win. (alludes to *Star Wars*)

When he saw her, an arrow pierced his heart and he fell. (alludes to Cupid)

Flee now; pray later. (In style, this should remind the reader of the familiar "Fly now; pay later" advertising slogan.)

The 1939 movie version of *The Wizard of Oz* is a popular source of allusion even today; note how the following examples recall scenes from the film:

"Toto, I have a feeling that we're not in Kansas any more."

"I could have clicked my heels together three times, but that would have put me in Kansas."—Robert Wagner dialog from *Love Among Thieves*

Here are three more examples of allusions:

"[Suddenly, hearing] a rustling behind me, I whirled, feeling like Stanley about to meet Livingston."—*Condé Nast Traveler*, July 1992

She played the perfect Barbie to his Ken.

Wipe that Cheshire cat grin off your face.

Analogy

An analogy is really only an extended metaphor or simile. It attempts to compare at length two objects from different classes; a classic analogy compares the human brain to a computer, for example, or the eye to a camera. Carried to its extreme, the comparison will be illogical because unlike objects can never be completely comparable.

Analogy, however, does help clarify your comparison; if appropriate and not far-fetched, it will help you to sustain a clarifying comparison through a short paragraph or even a long piece of prose. Analogies should help you to enrich your writing, to interpret some meaning or significance about your main points, to reflect your particular way of thinking about things, to add wit and charm to your style.

Examples

The New York Public Library might hold the key to your future; it unlocks many doors to knowledge; it opens the way to numerous opportunities. (This would be merely metaphor unless you extended it a little further.)

Life is like the movies: there are many kinds of plots, but you should be the director of your own script. (Does this suggest how you might discuss life as tragedy, comedy, melodrama, adventure?)

To the new student the college campus is like a forest—all trees, each indistinguishable from the other and each an obstacle in his or her path. (Extend this analogy by describing how the student finds the way through the "forest" and comes to know the name—and function—of each "tree.")

An *extended analogy* sustains a comparison for several sentences, at times even for a whole paragraph. Someone writing to clients in a business letter may use this writing technique effectively, as Margit White does in the following paragraph:

"Being invested in the stockmarkets is a little bit like being a surfer at the beach. Whether you have your money in a Mutual Fund of stocks, a diversified portfolio of individual stocks or a Quantum account, it is all the same. You spend a lot of time sitting on your surfboard bobbing up and down with the ebb and flow of small wavelets. But when the big wave comes, you are on your board positioned and ready for a glorious ride."—Prudential Securities *Client Letter*, January 1992

Now look at another analogy describing a landscape and comparing it to music. Does this analogy work? Can you see the comparisons suggested? What precise reaction do you have to this paragraph?

"It's a symphonic road, beginning with an andante among open hills, dropping into the somber adagio of the moist, dark redwood forest, winding its way back up through a scherzo of brighter glens and vales, and finally breaking into an allegro con brio climax of light, height, and distance, a counterpoint of long windy hill-sides, hemispheric silver-barked oaks, and miles of a vibrating sea."—Peter Garrison, "Riding the Edge," *Condé Nast Traveler*, September 1992

Checkpoint

✓ Never rely on an analogy as proof in logic or argument. An analogy is simply an imaginative comparison of two essentially different things.

Hyperbole and understatement

Two special types of irony—used in both prose and poetry—help communicate a message imaginatively: *hyperbole* (overstatement) and *litotes* (understatement). A bold, deliberately exaggerated statement is hyperbolic. It exaggerates the truth, but the writer does not expect the statement to be believed. Ironic in context, hyperbole can produce a fanciful effect or something comic or absurd. The speaker in Andrew Marvell's "To His Coy Mistress" uses hyperbole to present a "good line" to his beloved suggesting that if they had all the time in the world he would adore her patiently and lavishly:

> "An hundred years should go to praise / Thine eyes, and on thy forehead gaze; / Two hundred to adore each breast, / But thirty thousand to the rest."

Try adding a hyperbolic one-liner to add humor to your message. After six hours of steady rain, you might write, "Wonderful day, isn't it?" Or in describing a large cocktail party, you might try to impress your audience by recalling, "There were millions of people there, at least two hundred of my dearest, closest friends!"

By contrast, understatement deliberately says less than what you actually intend. The speaker or writer offers a message by stating the negative or opposite. This seeming contradiction produces an emphatic statement that is the heart of the message. Saying of a very wise person "She's no fool" helps stress the woman's intelligence through the understatement.

After describing a fine meal, you might underplay the excellence by saying "not bad." Note how Christopher Johns underplays the horror of a drink in which a poisonous snake floats:

> "A raw fish meal is called sashimi, and the ideal accompaniment to it is considered to be some double-distilled sake in the bottling of which a live Marmushi has been added. A Marmushi is a poisonous snake. I will spare the reader further details."—Christopher Johns, "Ah So!" The Journal of the International Wine and Food Society, February 1980

Irony

Irony conceals the intended meaning in words that convey the opposite meaning. It presents a discrepancy between the real and the intended. You have heard compliments that were actually veiled criticism; the tone of a speaker's delivery conveys the real meaning. Try pronouncing "He's no fool," to convey different meanings with different intonations. Ironical remarks are softer than harsher, sarcastic speech. In sarcasm both speaker and listener know the real meaning of the message; in irony the meaning is subtler and less biting.

In prose, irony can be a powerful weapon. Jonathan Swift expertly attacked the Irish Catholics in his ironical "A Modest Proposal." Here he presents a wholly unthinkable answer to overpopulation—that children of the Irish poor be sold, at the age of one year, to provide "a most delicious, nourishing, and wholesome food" for wealthy purchasers. Swift advances this suggestion in logic so rigid and technically flawless that readers, while outraged, find themselves reluctantly appreciating his closing statements:

> "I profess in the sincerity of my heart that I have not the least personal interest in endeavoring to promote this necessary work, having no other good than the public good of my country, by advancing our trade, providing for infants, relieving the poor, and giving some pleasure to the rich. I have no children by which I can propose to get a single penny; the youngest being nine years old, and my wife past childbearing."

Metaphor

With a metaphor you do not say that something is "like" or "as" another thing; you simply say that one thing IS something else. (A is B.)

As with similes, here again, the two things being compared must be unlike.

There are two types of metaphors.

TYPE 1:

The "A equals B" type uses two terms.

Her eyes are blue jewels.

The sun is a golden heater warming the land.

TYPE 2:

The single-word metaphor implies or suggests a comparison.

a. *verbs:* Almost any sports page will yield a rich harvest of these verbs with picture-making power.

The quarterback blasted through the line of San Francisco's defense.

The fans came unglued and jumped up in a frenzy of excitement.

Dr. J operated on his opponents in the NBA finals.

b. *nouns:* The image or picture of comparison is implied in a noun, which names one thing by calling it another.

When the news anchor was hired, the television producers thought she might be another loose cannon.

The Arkansas defensive lineup was a brick wall—impenetrable and invulnerable.

The quarterback crossed the line into the Promised Land, giving Ohio State six more points and a Rose Bowl win.

"Fashion is architecture: It is a matter of proportion."—Coco Chanel

c. *adjectives:* Adjectives may also imply comparisons; they describe something in terms that no reader should ever take literally.

Jennifer's purring hum and contented snuggle matched his image of her as a cat.

Every butchered sentence kills the meaning of your prose.

Checkpoint

✓ Don't "mix" your images in a metaphor. Look at these ghastly creations!

They stepped forth into the sea of matrimony and found it a very rocky road.

The "ship of state" might be off its keel; it might sink or flounder or get off course without a firm hand at the helm, but it could never bog down in a storm of red tape or be the leader of the team or surge ahead in second gear.

Personification

Used more frequently in poetry than in prose, personification gives human characteristics (such as weeping or laughing) to inanimate objects or abstractions. It gives them feelings or human attributes to create striking visual images. Abstract concepts, such as love, freedom, and time; things; or plants and flowers are often personified—Queen Anne's lace, baby's breath. Children's literature is full of personification—talking rabbits and bears and lions—Winnie the Pooh, the Cheshire Cat, the White Rabbit.

Examples

The cat said, "I want to go out."

The flower turned its face to the sun.

The rain sang on the roof.

"The dish ran away with the spoon."

Whispering mysteriously, the trees swayed in the forest.

Simile

A simile compares essentially unlike things. It says that two things are similar when they are not really alike at all. You need one of the following connectives in every simile: *like, as, than,* or a verb such as *seems.*

Examples

It's about as easy as striking a match on a mirror.

Since the disasters at the World Trade Center and the Pentagon, the threat of terrorism has roosted, like a vulture in a tree, in America's awareness.

The flowers spread over the hill like a colorful Persian carpet.

Here is an extended simile:

> "The oil boom is like a phone call from a lost and forgotten lover; not entirely welcome, a reminder of good times that turned sour, of the end of innocence, of harsh truths learned and years irretrievably gone, of how easy it is to make a terrible mistake and how foolish it is to think that things will last forever."—Paul Burka, "Boom Town," *Texas Monthly*, December 1992

In the following similes the writer uses objects to convey measurements and compare unlike things:

> "My solitude grew more and more obese, like a pig."—Mishima Yukio, *Temple of the Golden Pavilions*

> "The discriminating mind is a dancer and a magician with the objective world as his stage."—Lankeventara Sutra

FURTHER READING

If you need additional information or more complete descriptions of figurative language in poetry and prose, you may consult one of the following standard reference works:

Baldick, Chris. *The Concise Oxford Dictionary of Literary Terms.* Oxford: New York: Oxford University Press, 1990.

Beckson, Karl. *Literary Terms, A Dictionary*, 3rd ed. New York: Noonday Press, 1989.

Cuddon, J. A., and Claire Preston, eds., *The Penguin Dictionary of Literary Terms and Literary Theory*, 4th ed. New York: Penguin USA, 2000.

Hart, James D. (with revisions by Phillip W. Leininger). *The Oxford Companion to American Literature.* Oxford: New York: Oxford University Press, 1995.

Hunter, J. Paul. *The Norton Introduction to Poetry*, 4th ed. New York: Norton, 1991.

Kennedy, X. J. *Introduction to Poetry*, 10th ed. New York: Harper Collins, 2001.

Murphy, Bruce, ed. *Benet's Readers Encyclopedia*, 4th ed. New York: Harper Collins, 1996.

CHAPTER 5

The Twenty Patterns—In Print

Let's look at some examples of the patterns in complete works. We've noted the pattern numbers in the margins to help you see which pattern is used and how it enhances the writing.

TOUGH COUNTRY*

from *Tularosa* by C. L. Sonnichsen

SENTENCE
PATTERNS

The Tularosa country is a parched desert where everything, from cactus to cowman, carries a weapon of some sort, and the only creatures who sleep with both eyes closed are dead.   11

In all the sun-scorched and sand-blasted reaches of the Southwest there is no grimmer region. Only the fierce and the rugged can live here—prickly pear and mesquite; rattlesnake and tarantula. True, Texas cattlemen made the cow a native of the region seventy-five years ago, but she would have voted against the step if she had been asked.   14

10a

5

From the beginning this lonesome valley has been a laboratory for developing endurance, a stern school specializing in just one subject: the Science of Doing Without.   14

10

Everything has been done to promote the success of the experiments. There is almost no water; no

shade. High mountain walls all around keep out the   14 and 12
tenderfeet. On the west, screening off the Rio Grande
valley with its green fields and busy highways, great   5
ridges of limestone and granite—Franklin and Organ;
San Andres and Oscuro—heave and roll northward   7
from El Paso. Across the valley to the eastward, shut-   14
ting off the oases along the Pecos, the Hueco mountains merge with the pine-cloaked Sacramentos, and
these give way to Sierra Blanca and Jicarilla, with
12,000-foot Sierra Blanca Peak soaring in naked   12
majesty over all.

The Tularosa country lies between the ranges, a
great pocket of sand, sun, and sparse vegetation
thirty miles wide, more or less, and over two hundred
miles long. The Jumanos Mesa, named for a long-
vanished tribe of Indians, gives it a northern bound-   11
ary. To the south it merges with the Chihuahua
Desert which pushes far down into Mexico.

Seen from the tops of the screening ranges, it   12
looks like a flat, gray-green, sun-flooded expanse of   4
nothing, impressive only because the eye can travel a
hundred miles and more in one leap. Near at hand it   12
is full of surprises. The northern end of the valley is a
little less parched. Grass still grows tall on Carrizozo
Flat, and bean farmers have plowed up the country
around Claunch. Nearby, two prehistoric lava flows
cover the land with an appalling jumble of volcanic
rock known locally as the *malpais*.

South of the lava flows, the vast gypsum deposits
called the White Sands spread out in a deathly, glit-
tering world of pure white which edges eastward a
few inches each year, threatening in a few millennia   12
to swallow up everything as far as the Sacramentos.

Sometimes the valley floor heaves in sand dunes;   1
sometimes it breaks into red hummocks, each one   18
crowned with the delicate green leaves and lethal
thorns of a mesquite bush. There are broad swales
where the yuccas grow in groves—leprous alkali flats   4

where even the sturdy greasewood can barely hold its own—long inclines of tall grama grass where the foothills rise to the knees of the mountains—and countless acres of prickly pear and *lechuguilla* and rabbit brush.

4a

A harsh, forbidding country, appalling to new-comers from gentler regions. But it has its moments of intense beauty. Sunrise and sunset are magic times. Under a full moon, that lonely, whispering waste is transformed into an austere corner of fairyland. The belated traveler catches his breath when the tender fingers of dawn pick out the tiny black shapes of the pine trees far above him on the top of the Sacramentos. One does not forget the Organs black-ening against the sunset, swathed in a veil of lilac shadows—the eerie gleam of the white sands at moonrise—a swarthy cloud dissolving in a column of rain, the froth of impact showing white at its foot while all round the sun shines serenely on.

20
19

14

12
4 (with dashes)
12
18

The yucca is a thorny and cantankerous object, but in the spring it puts up a ten-foot stalk which explodes in a mass of creamy-white blossoms. And so it is with other sullen citizens of the desert when their time comes: the prickly pear with its rich yellow flower, the desert willow dripping with pendent pink and lavender, little pincushion cacti robing them-selves in mauve petals more gorgeous than roses, the ocotillo shrouding its savage spines in tiny green leaves till its snaky arms look like wands of green fur, each one tipped with a long finger of pure scarlet.

10

4

18

It is big country—clean country—and if it has no tenderness, it has strength and a sort of magnificence.

9
16a

To live there has always been a risky business—a matter not only of long chances and short shrifts but also of privation and danger. This was true of the pre-historic cave dwellers who lived only a little better than their animal neighbors in the Huecos many centuries gone by. It was true of the little pueblo

16 and 5
(Note repetition
of "true" in
parallel construction
here)

communities which grew up later in the mountain canyons and wherever a wet-weather lake made existence possible on the valley floor. It was true in historic times of the peaceful Christian Indians who abandoned their unfinished church at Gran Quivira when the Apaches overwhelmed them nearly three hundred years ago.

Yes, it has always been hard country—frontier country—and for obvious reasons, the first reason being those same Apaches. The slopes of the Sierra Blanca were their favorite haunts as far back as we have any records, and though they ranged far and wide over the desert and even moved to Mexico for decades when the Comanches descended upon them, they always came back to the mountain rivers and the tall pines. A merciless environment made them tough and almost unbeatable fighters. They kept their country to themselves as long as they were able, waging a never-ending war against hunger and thirst, Comanches and Mexicans, soldiers and settlers, until their power was broken less than a lifetime ago.

Highways and railroads were slow in coming to a region so far removed from the gathering places of men and money. Sheer isolation did what the Apache was not able to do alone: it held off the traders and developers for years while the Rio Grande and Pecos settlements were booming.

But the most potent force of all for keeping people out was plain, old-fashioned, skin-cracking drought. The rainfall was imperceptible, and there was just enough ground water available to cause trouble. On the valley floor there was next to none at all until men got around to drilling wells. A few springs existed here and there in the Organs and the San Andres, none of them big enough to supply more than a few men and beasts. The eastern mountains were higher and better supplied. Spring-fed streams

9

9 and 18

12 and 5

17

3

4

14

came down from the Sierra Blanca at Three Rivers,
while Tularosa Creek descended the pass between
Sierra Blanca and Sacramento beside the main trail
from the Pecos to the Rio Grande.

Farther south, where the mile-high cliffs of the   13
Sacramentos soar above the plain, a number of
canyons drained off the water from the heights—   10a
Dog Canyon and Agua Chiquita; Sacramento and   5
Grapevine. In Sacramento Canyon and in Dog
Canyon the water was more or less permanent. But
everywhere, until the skill and cupidity of man turned   13 and 14
the liquid gold to account, it flowed out onto the flats
a pitifully short distance and disappeared in the sand.
Along with it, as the years passed, flowed the blood   15a
of many a man who gave up his life for a trickle of
water.

Sensible men, cautious men, stayed away from   9a
such a place. But the adventurous and the hardy and   4a
the reckless kept on coming. Each one had a dream
of some sort—water for his cows, solitude for his   4
soul, gold to make him rich. For even the Tularosa
country has its treasures. The ghostly ruins of Gran
Quivira have been honeycombed by men obsessed
with the notion that the Indians buried a hoard of
gold before they left. At the northeast corner of the   14
valley, in the Jicarilla Mountains, lies the abandoned
gold camp of White Oaks, the site of rich mining   15a
properties seventy years ago. Midway between El
Paso and Alamogordo, on the rocky slopes of the
Jarillas, Orogrande sits solitary, remembering the   12
days when prospectors and miners swarmed in; and a
few miles away at the San Augustin Pass the abandoned shafts at Organ tell a similar tale.

But the real story of Tularosa is the story of Texas
cattlemen—drifting herdsmen who began to invade   10a
the valley in the early eighties, bringing their stern   12
folkways with them. They too ran into trouble, for

their law was not the law of the Mexicans or the
Indians or the Yankees who arrived during and after
the Civil War. It was those proud riders who kept the
Old West alive in that lonely land until yesterday. It
was the clash of their ways and standards with the
ways and standards of the settled citizens which
caused the feuds and killings and hatreds that make
up the unwritten history of the region. The Apaches
and the climate and the lay of the land helped. But
in the last analysis it was the Texans who made
Tularosa the Last of the Frontier West.

4a
Note parallel
"it was"
construction

9
4a

4a

Those times seem as remote from present-day
reality as the wars of Caesar and Charlemagne, but
they have left a brand on the soul of many a man and
woman still living. That is why this story has never
been fully told—why all of it can never be told. For
out here in the desert the West of the old days has
never quite given way to a newer America. Customs
have changed, but attitudes have held fast. To test
this fact, try asking questions about certain people
and events. Old men clam up and change the subject.
Young ones who have heard something hesitate a
long time before telling what they know about the
sins and tribulations of their grandfathers. Once it
was dangerous to talk about these things. Even now
it is not considered wise. The fears and loyalties and
customs of yesterday—these things still cast their
shadows on us who live on the edge of the desert. On
the streets of El Paso or Las Cruces or Alamogordo
you can still hear the click of bootheels belonging to
men who played their parts in dramas which would
make a Hollywood movie look tame. Their sons and
daughters still live among us—fine people, too—and
their friends still frown on loose discussion.

17
9a

19
4
6

14 and 6

7a

For these reasons this is not an easy story to tell,
but it is time someone told it. So let's go back to the
beginning, before the Texas cattle crowded in, ate

14

the grass down to the roots, and trampled the plain
into dust—back to the days when the country was the   9
way God made it: bunch grass growing up to a
horse's belly; miles of yellow flowers in the wet years;
little rainwater lakes at the foot of the Organs and   4
the San Andres, long since dried out and buried in   12
dust; sun and sand and sixty long miles to town.   4a

EXCERPT FROM *A THOUSAND DAYS**

Arthur M. Schlesinger, Jr.

	SENTENCE PATTERNS

After Kennedy's death, Adlai Stevenson called him the "contemporary man." His youth, his vitality, his profound modernity—these were final elements in his power and potentiality as he stood on the brink of the Presidency. For Kennedy was not only the first President to be born in the twentieth century. More than that, he was the first representative in the White House of a distinctive generation, the generation which was born during the First World War, came of age during the depression, fought in the Second World War and began its public career in the atomic age.

> 14
> 4 and 9a
> 6
>
> 9

This was the first generation to grow up as the age of American innocence was coming to an end. To have been born nearly a decade earlier, like Lyndon Johnson, or nearly two decades earlier, like Adlai Stevenson, was to be rooted in another and simpler America. Scott Fitzgerald had written that his contemporaries grew up "to find all Gods dead, all wars fought, all faiths in man shaken." But the generation which came back from the Second World War found that gods, wars, and faiths in man had, after all, survived if in queer and somber ways. The realities of the twentieth century which had shocked their fathers now wove the fabric of their own lives. Instead of reveling in being a lost generation, they set out in one mood or another to find, if not themselves, a still point in the turning world. The predicament was even worse for the generation which had been too young to fight in the war, too young to recall the age of innocence, the generation which had experienced nothing but turbulence. So in the fifties some

> 11
> 11
>
> 9a
>
> 4
>
> 14
>
> 9a
> 9

---

sought security at the expense of identity and became organization men. Others sought identity at
the expense of security and became beatniks. Each
course created only a partial man. There was need for
a way of life, a way of autonomy, between past and
present, the organization man and the anarchist, the
square and the beat.

It was autonomy which this humane and self-
sufficient man seemed to embody. Kennedy simply
could not be reduced to the usual complex of socio-
logical generalizations. He was Irish, Catholic, New
England, Harvard, Navy, Palm Beach, Democrat, and
so on; but no classification contained him. He had
wrought an individuality which carried him beyond
the definitions of class and race, region and religion.
He was a free man, not just in the sense of the cold-
war cliché, but in the sense that he was, as much as
man can be, self-determined and not the servant of
forces outside him.

This sense of wholeness and freedom gave him an
extraordinary appeal not only to his own generation
but even more to those who came after, the children
of turbulence. Recent history had washed away
the easy consolations and the old formulas. Only a
few things remained on which contemporary man
could rely, and most were part of himself—family,
friendship, courage, reason, jokes, power, patriotism.
Kennedy demonstrated the possibility of the new self-
reliance. As he had liberated himself from the past,
so he had liberated himself from the need to rebel
against the past. He could insist on standards, admire
physical courage, attend his church, love his father
while disagreeing with him, love his country without
self-doubt or self-consciousness. Yet, while absorbing
so much of the traditional code, his sensibility was
acutely contemporaneous. He voiced the disquietude
of the postwar generation—the mistrust of rhetoric,
the disdain for pomposity, the impatience with the

Note parallel
construction

19
9
5

5
16

16

10a
4

16

4 (verbs in
series)

10a

postures and pieties of other days, the resignation to
disappointment. And he also voiced the new generation's longings—for fulfillment in experience, for
the subordination of selfish impulses to higher ideals,
for a link between past and future, for adventure and
valor and honor. What was forbidden were poses,
histrionics, the heart on the sleeve and the tongue on
the cliché. What was required was a tough, non-
chalant acceptance of the harsh present and an open
mind toward the unknown future.

This was Kennedy, with his deflationary war-time
understatement (when asked how he became a hero,
he said, "It was involuntary. They sank my boat");
his contempt for demagoguery (once during the
campaign, after Kennedy had disappointed a Texas
crowd by his New England restraint, Bill Attwood
suggested that next time he wave his arms in the air
like other politicians; Kennedy shook his head and
wrote—he was saving his voice—"I always swore
one thing I'd never do is—" and drew a picture of a
man waving his arms in the air); his freedom from
dogma, his appetite for responsibility, his instinct for
novelty, his awareness and irony and control; his
imperturbable sureness in his own powers, not because he considered himself infallible, but because,
given the fallibility of all men, he supposed he could
do the job as well as anyone else; his love of America
and pride in its traditions and ideals.

Margin annotations:

4

4a

parallel
construction
with pattern
17

19

1

4
and
4a

16

Time named Charles Kuralt "the laureate of the common man." He has the poet's gift for describing the infinite diversity of America and Americans. As you read the essay that follows, become aware of his passion for his subject and the grace and effortlessness of his style. Think about how Kuralt blends a variety of rhetorical tools into the paragraphs, matching and coordinating his rhetoric with his troubled message.

1. Analyze Kuralt's paragraphs and try to identify familiar sentence patterns. In particular, look for combinations of other sentence patterns.

2. Next, look for patterns that appeal to you. Try to imitate some of them and adapt them to your own writing.

3. Pay close attention to the striking images Kuralt creates with his vivid language. Note how the immediacy of his descriptions makes historical figures come to life.

PLACE OF SORROWS*
(*Little Big Horn, Montana*)

Charles Kuralt

This is about a place where the wind blows and the grass grows and a river flows below a hill. Nothing is here but the wind and the grass and the river. But of all the places in America, this is the saddest place I know.

The Indians called the river the Greasy Grass. White men called it the Little Big Horn. From a gap in the mountains to the east, Brevet Major General George A. Custer's proud Seventh Cavalry came riding, early in the morning of June 25th, 1876, riding toward the Little Big Horn.

Custer sent one battalion, under Major Marcus Reno, across the river to attack what he thought might be a small village of hostile Sioux. His own battalion he galloped behind the ridges to ride down on the village from the rear. When at last Custer brought his two hundred and thirty-one troops to the top of a hill and looked down toward the river, what he saw was an encampment of fifteen thousand Indians stretching for two and a half miles, the largest assembly of Indians the plains had ever known—and a thousand mounted warriors coming straight for him.

Reno's men, meantime, had been turned, routed, chased across the river, joined by the rest of the regiment, surrounded, and now were dying, defending a nameless brown hill.

In a low, protected swale in the middle of their narrowing circle, the one surviving doctor improvised a field hospital and did what he could for the wounded. The grass covers the place now and grows in the shallow rifle trenches above, which were dug that day by knives and tin cups and fingernails.

Two friends in H Company, Private Charles Windolph and Private Julian Jones, fought up here, side by side, all that day, and stayed awake all that night, talking, both of them scared. Charles Windolph said: "The next morning when the firing commenced, I said to Julian, 'We'd better get our coats off.' He didn't move. I looked at him. He was shot through the heart." Charles Windolph won the Congressional Medal of Honor up here, survived, lived to be ninety-eight. He didn't die until 1950. And never a day passed in all those years that he didn't think of Julian Jones.

---

*Reprinted by permission of The Putnam Publishing Group from *On the Road with Charles Kuralt* by Charles Kuralt. Copyright © 1985 by CBS, Inc.

And Custer's men, four miles away? There are stones in the grass that tell the story of Custer's men. The stones all say the same things: "U.S. soldier, Seventh Cavalry, fell here, June 25, 1876."

The warriors of Sitting Bull, under the great Chief Gall, struck Custer first and divided his troops. Two Moon and the northern Cheyenne struck him next. And when he tried to gain a hilltop with the last remnants of his command, Crazy Horse rode over that hill with hundreds of warriors and right through his battalion.

The Indians who were there later agreed on two things: that Custer and his men fought with exceeding bravery; and that after half an hour, not one of them was alive.

The Army came back that winter—of course, the Army came back—and broke the Sioux and the Cheyenne and forced them back to the starvation of the reservations and, in time, murdered more old warriors and women and children on the Pine Ridge Reservation than Custer lost young men in battle here.

That's why this is the saddest place. For Custer and the Seventh Cavalry, courage only led to defeat. For Crazy Horse and the Sioux, victory only led to Wounded Knee.

Come here sometime, and you'll see. There is melancholy in the wind and sorrow in the grass, and the river weeps.

Appendix

PUNCTUATION

Why punctuate?

Most readers expect certain signals to conform to standard conventions. We would be confused by this:

> denrael evah lla dluoc eW
> sdrawkcab sdrow daer ot
> tes dah sretnirp ylrae fi
> yaw taht epyt rieht
>
> upside-down is really no trick at all.
> and most people find that reading

We also know the shapes of printed words so well that

we can read almost anything when only the tops of letters show

but we have more difficulty when we can see only the bottoms.

The same kind of training has made us come to expect that printed words today will have spaces between them even though in many early writings allthewordsrantogetherwithoutspacesanywherenoteven betweensentencesandtherewerenosuchthingsasparagraphs.

In the same way, we expect punctuation will follow conventions just as we expect to read from left to right and to find spaces between words. We also expect punctuation marks to signal something about the relationships of words to each other after all the same arrangement of words for example Joe said Henry is a dirty slob can have two different meanings depending on the punctuation even a few marks to signal the end of each sentence would have helped you in this paragraph to help

Format for this page was partly suggested by John Spradley's article—"The Agenwit of Inpoint"—in JETT (*Journal of English Teaching Techniques*), Spring, 1971, pages 23–31.

your reader give him some of the conventional signals we call punctuation marks.

Punctuation: a signal system

In the American English sentence, punctuation presents a set of signal systems for the readers. If your code is clear, the reader will get your signals. If it is faulty, the reader will be confused and you will have failed to communicate. Some marks guide the eye; others, the ear, that is, they indicate the mental intonation (pause, stress, pitch) the reader should use. For instance, the period signals a full stop with pitch of voice dropped to indicate a long pause, whereas an exclamation point "shouts" and implies the raising of the writer's voice. The period indicates a long pause, the comma indicates a short pause. The semicolon signals not only a stop but also "equality": Something equally structured will follow. The colon signals that the thought is not complete, that something explanatory will follow: an important word, phrase, sentence, or a formal listing. The colon is a very formal mark, the dash is less formal, and material within parentheses just "whispers" to the reader. Generally speaking, these marks are not interchangeable; each has its own function to perform. Therefore, you need to learn when to use the following punctuation marks.

BRACKETS

1. to enclose additions, corrections, or other changes made in original quoted material

   "Henry's traffic ticket in London cost him fifteen pounds [$30]," Molly had written in her diary.

2. to alert the reader to an error in quoted material. Use brackets around the Latin term *sic* (meaning "so" or "thus") to indicate the error in the quoted passage, such as an incorrect name, date, or spelling.

   "Because Meryl was trying to loose [*sic*] weight, she was to [*sic*] ill to go to the wedding," Jim wrote in his letter.

The United States Postal Service now requires standardized addressing forms that can be scanned by computers and thus move the mail faster and more reliably. These new forms challenge traditional punctuation protocols by omitting commas and periods. Here are the seven guidelines for standardized addressing:

1. Always put the addressee's name on the first line. (If you are sending mail to someone at a company, put the company name on the second line.)

2. In addition to the street address or post office box number, include the following if appropriate:

   N (North), S (South), E (East), W (West), NE, NW, SE, SW.

3. Use the following abbreviations: AVE (Avenue), ST (Street), DR (Drive), RD (Road), PL (Place), CIR (Circle), BLVD (Boulevard), CT (Court), RM (Room), STE (Suite), or APT (Apartment) number.

4. Put the zip code after the city and state and on the same line. If you know the ZIP + 4 code, use it.

5. Capitalize and left-justify all lines. Do not punctuate.

6. Always include the return address.

7. Use standard state abbreviations: CA for California, ME for Maine, and so on (with no periods).

COLON: to call attention to what follows

1. before a list that follows a complete statement

   Sara bought several items for her upcoming cruise: a bikini, a cocktail dress, and two pairs of metallic sandals.

2. before an independent clause that restates, in different form, the idea of the preceding independent clause (in a compound sentence)

   A lizard never worries about losing its tail: it can always grow another.

3. after the words "following," "as follows," or "thus"

   On her trip Sara planned to take the following: the newest Tom Clancy thriller, her brother's Nikon camera, and a stuffed cosmetic case.

4. before a climactic appositive at the end of the sentence

   The grasping of seaweeds reveals the most resourceful part of the sea horse: its prehensile tail.

COMMAS: to separate main sentence elements

1. between independent clauses joined by coordinating conjunctions (*FANBOYS—for, and, nor, but, or, yet, so* only for clarity)

   I escaped from the burning house but I lost many dear treasures from the past. (needs no comma)

2. between elements of a series

   The produce counter had several varieties of lettuce, such as butter, romaine, red tip and iceberg. (The comma after the last item in the series before the conjunction—*red tip*—is now considered optional in journalistic and business writing.) But—

He used sage, chicken stock, cornbread and bread crumbs, and onions in the turkey stuffing. (With two "ands" here, the reader may get confused, so you need the comma after the last item in the series before the conjunction—*crumbs.*)

3. between contrasted elements in a "this, not that" construction

The criminal seemed smug and defiant about his despicable act, neither sorry nor repentant.

4. before direct quotations (such constructions as *he said, she answered,* and so on)

The politician said, "Yes, you must pay more taxes for Social Security."

5. between elements in dates, addresses, place names

Our new house is at 18 Denning Road, Hampstead, London NW3P 1SU England.

6. after a long introductory phrase or an adverbial clause preceding the main clause

If I buy too many municipal bonds, I may have less capital once interest rates begin to rise.

7. before an inverted element

The Tin Lizzie may have been dependable, but quiet it wasn't.

8. after any element that might be misread or might otherwise seem to run together

Once inside, the dog began to jump and bark.

9. in place of omitted words in elliptical constructions

A red light means stop; a green light, go.

10. after an absolute construction at the beginning of a sentence; before an absolute construction at the end

She sank back on her bed, her eyes filling with tears, her mouth grimacing in pain.

COMMAS: a pair to enclose

1. any interrupting construction between subject and verb, verb and object or complement, or any other two elements not normally separated

The weight of the prize-winning marlin, give or take a few ounces, was about 126 pounds.

2. a short appositive

The largest California vintner, the Gallo Company, has begun producing a new boutique wine, a Cabernet.

3. a noun or pronoun of direct address

Hey, you, get out of my way!

4. a nonrestrictive (*not* essential) interrupting modifier

Trisha's Victorian apartment, which I rented last summer, had mice in the pantry.

5. an absolute construction within a sentence

A break in the weather, God willing, is expected next week.

6. any parenthetical expression within a sentence

The understudy for the role, on the other hand, wanted as much money as the star.

DASH: to separate sentence elements

1. before a summary word to separate an introductory series of appositives from the independent clause

Catwoman, Superman, Frankenstein's monster—all of these characters wore unusual costumes.

2. before an emphatic appositive at the end of a sentence

The kangaroo carries its own nest—its pouch.

3. occasionally before a repetition for emphasis

The plumber came into the kitchen loaded—loaded with tools, not beer.

DASH: a pair to enclose

1. an internal series

Three basic fencing moves—the advance, the retreat, the lunge—demand careful balance by both fencers.

2. an abrupt change in thought or a pronounced sentence interrupter

There's a great website—I can't remember the URL—to help you solve that problem.

3. a parenthetical element, often for emphasis

   Her recent behavior—however bizarre—must be judged with compassion.

4. an interrupting modifier or appositive for dramatic effect

   J. K. Rowling's popular novel—*Harry Potter and the Sorcerer's Stone*, atop the best-seller list for weeks—became a popular film.

EXCLAMATION POINT

1. after a phrase or sentence expressing intense emotion

   "So what!" Eric yelled contemptuously.

2. after a strong interjection

   I just won $10,000!

PARENTHESES: a pair to enclose

1. words, phrases, expressions, or complete sentences that have no bearing upon the main idea (to make asides or "whispers" to the reader)

   I told Alice (who wouldn't?) the truth.

2. an interrupting series

   The colors of the flag (red, white, and blue) lavishly decorated the convention center.

3. an appositive

   His former wife (once a famous Philadelphia model) now owns a well-known boutique in the Bahamas.

4. an interrupting modifier between subject and verb

   The slogan of the state (comical yet enticing) helps promote tourism and a cleaner environment.

PERIOD

1. at the end of a declarative sentence

   I enjoy creating new sentence patterns.

2. after an abbreviation

   CAUTION: Remember to put periods after abbreviations, such as Mr., St., and Sept.

3. three spaced periods to indicate an ellipsis (where something has been left out)

The fourth graders raced through "I pledge allegiance . . . with liberty and justice for all" in thirty seconds.

QUESTION MARK

1. at the end of a direct question

Did you see that tattoo on Tommy's arm?

2. after each question in a series

Where are the jewels? the crown? the rings? the tiaras?

3. in parentheses to express uncertainty

In 742 (?) Charlemagne was born.

NOTE: Do not use a question mark to indicate

    a. intended irony: His humorous letter failed to amuse her.
    b. an indirect question: Joe asked when we were going to have chiles rellenos again.
    c. a courteous request: Will you please pass the butter.

QUOTATION MARKS

1. ALWAYS AFTER periods and commas

"I am not European," she said indignantly. "I am a U.S. citizen."

2. ALWAYS BEFORE colons and semicolons

Read James Joyce's short story "Araby"; learn what it's like to be disappointed in love.

Laura won an unexpected prize for her science-fair project, "Lumitox and the Environment": an all-expense-paid trip to Stockholm to attend the Nobel Prize ceremonies.

3. before or after question marks and exclamation points, depending upon the context of the sentence

James asked, "Can you meet me at seven o'clock?"

Did James say, "Meet me at seven o'clock"?

4. to enclose the actual words of a speaker

"Ask not what your country can do for you; ask what you can do for your country."

5. To identify symbols, letters, and words used as such

   (He had too many "buts" in this paragraph, and his "$" sign is a simple "s.")

NOTE: In type, a word used as such is usually set in italics: too many *buts*.

6. to enclose the titles of short stories, short poems, paintings, songs, magazine articles, essays, and chapters of books, BUT NOT book titles

   William Butler Yeats's "Leda and the Swan" and Correggio's painting "Leda" dramatize an erotic event that ultimately led to the Trojan war.

NOTE: In type the titles of works of art are often set in italics: Correggio's painting *Leda*.

SEMICOLON: to separate important sentence elements

1. between independent clauses in a compound sentence without a conjunction

   You'd better read this e-mail; I think you need to answer it now.

2. between independent clauses in a compound sentence with a conjunction when there are commas in one or both clauses

   Sara has received an invitation to the Spanish ambassador's reception; she looks forward to dancing, but she will be disappointed if she can't try out the salsa, flamenco, or merengue.

3. before transitional connectives (conjunctive adverbs: *however, therefore, furthermore, thus, hence, likewise, moreover, nonetheless, nevertheless*) separating two independent clauses

   The race riot brought no peace to the city; nonetheless, it did force groups who had resisted before to talk to one another.

4. between items in a series containing internal commas

   Jason had to complete several projects due at the end of the semester: a journal, which he hadn't kept up; a science experiment, which was only half finished; and a research paper, which he had almost completed.

SUGGESTED REVIEW QUESTIONS

PATTERN
NUMBERS

I and 3

1. Explain the difference between a compound sentence with a semicolon and one with a colon. What is the specific difference in the second clause?

2

2. What kind of verb must be "understood" in the second clause before you can omit it?

   Can you ever omit something other than the verb in an elliptical construction?

4–8

3. What kinds of things can be listed in series?

   What slots in the sentence can contain series?

   Explain the patterns and the punctuation for the different kinds of series.

4. In PATTERN 6, what two things come immediately after the series of appositives?

5. Why must the series in PATTERN 7 be set off by a pair of dashes?

   What other marks of punctuation might occasionally substitute for those dashes?

6. In what two particular places in an essay would PATTERN 8 be good to use? What should go into the dependent clause?

7. What other patterns can perform the same function?

8. What qualifications should a word have before you put it in PATTERN 9?

9a

9. What kinds of words can you repeat in parallel structure? In what slots might they appear?

10. What kind of construction must come after the comma to keep PATTERN 9 from becoming a PATTERN 1 with a comma splice?

10 and 10a

11. Write one sentence three times, using different punctuation marks before the appositive (comma, dash, colon). Then explain the difference in

emphasis that the punctuation creates. Which is least emphatic? Which is most emphatic? Which makes a longer pause? Which is most formal?

12. What besides a single word can be an appositive?

13. *a.* What is the difference between the construction following the colon in PATTERN 3 and the one following the colon in PATTERN 10?

    b. What is the difference between the construction following the dash in PATTERN 9 and the one following the dash in PATTERN 10a?

7a and 11

14. Explain the difference between an internal appositive and an interrupting modifier.

15. In PATTERN 11, what two main parts of the sentence are separated by the interrupting modifier?

11

16. What three marks of punctuation can separate an interrupting modifier from the rest of the sentence? Can you ever use just ONE of these marks?

17. Write the same sentence three times. Punctuate it with a pair of commas, a pair of dashes, and a pair of parentheses; then explain the difference in sound and emphasis in each.

11a

18. Write a sentence that functions as an interrupting modifier in another sentence.

11a

19. Write a question as an interrupting modifier. Where does the question mark go?

12

20. Where do participles come from? How are they always used? What different kinds of endings may they have?

21. How can you avoid a dangling participle in PATTERN 12?

22. What kind of modifier needs a comma after it in PATTERN 13?

14

23. What does "inverted sentence" mean?

PATTERN
NUMBERS

19a	40. Where are good places to use a short question in writing?
20	41. What two reasons may make a writer use a deliberate fragment?
20	42. What is the importance of the surrounding context for a deliberate fragment?
20	43. What different kinds of functions may the fragment perform?

MISCELLANEOUS QUESTIONS
(for class discussion or essay tests)

1. Write the same sentence twice and punctuate it two different ways. Discuss the difference in sound, emphasis, and effect.

2. Write a sentence with S—V—DO. Now put the DO in a different place and notice the effect.

3. Discuss how the same idea can be expressed with different kinds of phrasing, as in the following examples:

   Bad grades bother John.

   What bothers John is bad grades.

   John is bothered by bad grades.

   John, bothered by bad grades, decided to burn some midnight oil.

   Are bad grades bothering John?

   Bad grades having bothered him before, John determined that this semester would be different.

4. Make up some sentences with nonsense words and discuss the structure and punctuation involved.

5. Define certain terms that occur in CHAPTER 2: *elliptical, appositive, parallel, construction, participle, absolute construction, series, modifier.*

6. What function does punctuation play in most sentences?

7. Why are style and variety in your sentence structure so important?

Index